SPECULATION, TRADING, AND BUBBLES

KENNETH J. ARROW LECTURE SERIES

KENNETH J. ARROW LECTURE SERIES

Kenneth J. Arrow's work has shaped the course of economics for the past sixty years so deeply that, in a sense, every modern economist is his student. His ideas, style of research, and breadth of vision have been a model for generations of the boldest, most creative, and most innovative economists. His work has yielded such seminal theorems as general equilibrium, social choice, and endogenous growth, proving that simple ideas have profound effects. The Kenneth J. Arrow Lecture Series highlights economists, from Nobel laureates to groundbreaking younger scholars, whose work builds on Arrow's scholarship as well as his innovative spirit. The books in the series are an expansion of the lectures that are held in Arrow's honor at Columbia University.

Creating a Learning Society: A New Approach to Growth, Development, and Social Progress, Joseph E. Stiglitz and Bruce C. Greenwald
The Arrow Impossibility Theorem, Eric Maskin and Amartya Sen

SPECULATION, TRADING, AND BUBBLES

JOSÉ A. SCHEINKMAN

WITH

**KENNETH J. ARROW,
PATRICK BOLTON,
SANFORD J. GROSSMAN,
AND JOSEPH E. STIGLITZ**

COLUMBIA UNIVERSITY PRESS | NEW YORK

Columbia University Press

Publishers Since 1893

New York   Chichester, West Sussex

cup.columbia.edu

Copyright © 2014 Columbia University Press

All rights reserved

Library of Congress Cataloging-in-Publication Data
Scheinkman, José Alexandre.
Speculation, trading, and bubbles / José A. Scheinkman, with
Kenneth J. Arrow, Patrick Bolton, Sanford J. Grossman,
and Joseph E. Stiglitz.
pages cm. — (Kenneth J. Arrow lecture series)
Includes bibliographical references and index.
ISBN 978-0-231-15902-9 (cloth : alk. paper) —
ISBN 978-0-231-53763-6 (ebook)
1. Speculation—History. 2. Investments—History. 3. Capital
market—History. 4. Stocks—Prices—History. I. Title.
HG6005.S34 2014
332.64'5—dc23
2014006646

CONTENTS

FOREWORD

KENNETH J. ARROW

I want to briefly express my gratitude for the existence of this series of lectures in my honor and to mark briefly the continuities and discontinuities in economics at Columbia.

Columbia was a very chaotic place when I was here. The departments were teaching different courses that had very little relation to each other. I came in really to study statistics, not to study economics. There was no degree in statistics, so I took my Ph.D. in economics simply as the only way of getting close to it. I got hooked. My mentor was somebody whose influence is still felt today, Harold Hotelling. I took his course in economics, which was totally different because nobody was teaching optimization, classic principles, or equilibrium; these subjects that were on the whole not taught. In fact, there was no course in price theory required of economics graduate students.

The "leading people" during this time were interested in business cycles, a term that is a little archaic now. Although that term is little used today, the ups and downs are still with us. The great man in that field was Wesley Clair Mitchell, a name that may mean very little to you, but he was the founder of the National Bureau of Economic Research. He was on leave in the year I was taking most of my courses, so he had a substitute, his deputy, Arthur F. Burns, who was a professor at Rutgers and who later became the chairman of the Federal Reserve and chairman of the Council of Economic Advisors. Burns was a very brilliant person, although I think he has had very little influence because he was very self-critical, and never really finished very much. But he was one of the brightest people I ever met, although his philosophy could not have been more opposed to mine. Even as a statistician, I wanted a formal model, and the models that I was attracted to were anything but. Many were based on the fact that the economy fluctuated a great deal. In retrospect, I am a little surprised that the financial side, which this volume discusses, did not play a role, considering all the ups and downs in the iron and steel industry. But all industries looked more or less alike to these people. As a statistician I did not want to be too critical, because the one thing that they were motivated to do was collect a lot of data, which I assumed the more formal econometricians would be then able to use, so one didn't want to discourage this activity.

The department, of course, has gone through so many changes; even after I returned after World War II, it was different. Albert Jay Nock very much emphasized imperfections in the credit market. He was the biggest figure in the postwar period. He and I respected each other a great deal. He was very encouraging to me even though he was going in a somewhat different direction. The subsequent history of the Economics Department has shown that it has continued, and perhaps even with increased vitality. The training of graduate students of economics at Columbia University and elsewhere is much more stringent and demanding than it was in my day. There is hardly any comparison. I want to welcome José Scheinkman to continue this tradition.

ACKNOWLEDGMENTS

The Kenneth J. Arrow Lecture Series has been made possible through the efforts of Columbia University's Committee on Global Thought (which I chaired when this series was inaugurated, and which is now co-chaired by Saskia Sassen) and by the Program in Economic Research (PER) of the Department of Economics at Columbia University (chaired by Michael Woodford at the time of this lecture) with the support and encouragement of the Columbia University Press.

We are especially indebted to Robin Stephenson and Sasha de Vogel of the Committee on Global Thought, and Myles Thompson and Bridget Flannery-McCoy of the Press for guiding this series to publication. We also thank Ryan Rivera and Laurence Wilse-Samson for their assistance with this volume.

Joseph E. Stiglitz

SPECULATION,
TRADING,
AND
BUBBLES

INTRODUCTION

JOSEPH E. STIGLITZ

Kenneth Arrow is one of Columbia's most distinguished graduates, whose accomplishments I hope all our graduate students seek to emulate. In this series, we have organized an annual lecture each around one of his papers or contributions. The lectures and subsequent discussions highlight the ideas that have been developed in subsequent decades elaborating on his original thoughts.

The first lecture, by Bruce Greenwald and me (with Philippe Aghion, Robert Solow, and Kenneth Arrow as discussants) was based on a paper Ken wrote in 1962 on learning by doing, which has been one of the most innovative papers in the theory of technical change. Arrow had explained how knowledge is developed in the process of production. Bruce and I expanded on that idea to enquire into how one could create a society that was better at learning–a society and an economy which would, accordingly, be more dynamic, with a faster pace of increases in standards of living. We developed that lecture into a book, *Creating a Learning Society: A New Approach to Growth, Development, and Social Progress.*

Amartya Sen and Eric Maskin delivered the second lecture, with Robert Solow and Ken as discussants, focusing on Ken's brilliant Ph.D. thesis, published as *Social Choice and Individual Values* (1951). This, the second volume of the Arrow lecture series, is titled *The Arrow Impossibility Theorem*, and includes additional papers and an introduction by Prasanta K. Pattanaik.

For the third lecture, we were pleased to have José Scheinkman speak on speculative trading and bubbles. His lecture was related to one of Ken's important contributions to the theory of general equilibrium. In the years since he delivered the lecture, he has revised his remarks and developed them into the impressive paper contained in this volume.

One of the most important ideas in economics is that of Adam Smith's invisible hand: the individuals are led, as if by an invisible hand, in the pursuit of their own self-interest, to the well-being of society as a whole. Though Smith enunciated this idea in 1776, it was not clear either the sense in which this was true (i.e., what was meant by the well-being of society) or the conditions under which it was true. To assess that, one had to construct a "model" of how the entire economy worked. Leon Walras, a great French mathematical economist, developed such a model in the late nineteenth century. A great Italian economist of the early twentieth century, Vilfredo Pareto, articulated what might be meant by maximizing societal well-being, a concept subsequently referred to as "Pareto Optimality," a situation in which no one could be made better off without making someone else worse off.

Walras described the competitive market equilibrium as a set of equations, one for each good (factor, service), equating demand and supply. The solution to this set of equations was referred to as the "general equilibrium" of the economy. But Walras left unresolved two questions. One was more technical: under what conditions would there exist a solution to this set of equations. In 1954, Arrow and Debreu provided the answer, building on work of Abraham Wald in the 1930s.

The far more important question was, under what conditions were competitive markets Pareto Optimal. In his classic 1951 paper, Arrow provided an answer (see also Debreu). One critical condition related to the nature of capital and risk markets: to establish Pareto optimality, one had to have a complete set of securities for insuring risk in every contingency in every period. These securities that promised to pay, say, a dollar if state i in date t were subsequently labeled Arrow-Debreu securities. This literature was the foundation of all modern finance theory. The equilibrium theory described what happened when markets worked well. As we have just seen in the last couple of years, markets do not always work well. Trying to understand why markets often don't work and what happens when financial markets in particular do not work well has been one of the major focal points of research since Ken's seminal work a half century ago.

For instance, when I was a graduate student, trying to understand if you could get efficient markets in the absence of a complete set of Arrow-Debreu securities was one of the real areas of interest. There was an important paper in 1967 by Peter Diamond, providing a set of conditions under which markets were still Pareto-efficient, or a constrained Pareto-efficient, even when there was not a full set of Arrow-Debreu securities. Then it was shown that that result depended on there being only one commodity—a little technicality, but one which limited the relevance of that to the real world (Stiglitz, 1982, Greenwald and Stiglitz, 1986).

Much of the research of the past forty years has focused on assessing market behavior in the presence of rational expectations, where individuals use all available information to make inferences about the future, and in which all individuals share the same beliefs. And much of the literature has focused on situations where, even though there may not be a complete set of markets, there are not constraints, such as on short sales. In practice, of course, individuals do differ in their beliefs. That this is so, and that this could have profound implications, I had suggested in an article some forty years ago (Stiglitz, 1972). But the full consequences of this become clear only when one imposes constraints on short sales, as Scheinkman demonstrates in this brilliant lecture.

At the time he gave the lecture, José was the Theodore A. Wells Professor of Economics at Princeton University. He is now Edwin W. Rickert Professor of Economics at Columbia University.

José's paper is followed by the adapted transcripts of the discussions that took place at the time of the lecture. First, Patrick Bolton is a member of the Committee on Global Thought and the Barbara and David Zalaznick Professor of Business and Professor of Economics, at Columbia. Second, Sanford Grossman taught at Stanford University with me in the mid-1970s and subsequently taught at Princeton, Chicago, and the University of Pennsylvania. He is now Chairman and Chief Executive Officer of QFS Asset Management.

As in the case of our other Arrow lectures, we have had the pleasure of drawing upon the large number of distinguished scholars who have been colleagues and students of Ken, many participating in the annual summer workshop at Stanford of the Institute of Mathematical Studies in the Social Sciences (IMSSS), in which Ken played such a pivotal role.

SPECULATION, TRADING, AND BUBBLES

JOSÉ A. SCHEINKMAN[*]

T he history of financial markets is strewn with periods in which asset prices seem to vastly exceed fundamentals— events commonly called bubbles. Nonetheless, there is very little agreement among economists on the economic forces that generate such occurrences. Numerous academic papers and books have been written explaining why the prices attained in a particular episode can be justified by economic actors rationally discounting future streams of payoffs. Some proponents of the efficient-markets theory even deny that one can attach any meaning to bubbles.[1]

[*] I wish to thank the Committee on Global Thought for the extraordinary honor of delivering this Arrow Lecture. Kenneth Arrow was the towering researcher in economic theory during the second half of the twentieth century, and the pricing of financial assets is one of the many topics in which his influence is deeply felt. I also want to thank Ken Arrow, Patrick Bolton, Sandy Grossman, Joe Stiglitz and members of the audience for comments during the lecture; Glen Weyl and Wei Xiong for comments on an earlier draft; and Matthieu Gomez and Michael D. Sockin for excellent research assistance. Many of the ideas developed in this lecture originated in joint research with Harrison Hong and Wei Xiong.

Part of the difficulty stems from the fact that economists' discussions of bubbles often concentrate solely on the behavior of asset prices. The most common definition of a bubble is "a period in which prices exceed fundamental valuation." Valuation, however, depends on a view of fundamentals, and efficient-market advocates correctly point out that valuations are almost always, ex post, wrong. In addition, bubbles are frequently associated with periods of technological or financial innovations that are of uncertain value at the time of the bubble, making it possible, although often unreasonable, to argue that buyers were paying a price that corresponded to a fair valuation of future dividends, given the information at their disposal.

In this lecture I adopt an alternative approach. I start with a more precise model of asset prices that allows for divergence between asset prices and fundamental valuation and that has additional implications that are easier to evaluate empirically. The model is based on the presence of fluctuating heterogeneous beliefs among investors and the existence of an asymmetry between the cost of acquiring an asset and the cost of shorting that same asset. The two basic assumptions of the model—differences in beliefs and higher costs of going short—are far from being standard in the literature on asset pricing. For many types of assets, including stocks, there are good economic reasons why investors should have more difficulty going short than going long, but most economic models assume no asymmetry. The existence of differences in beliefs is thought to be obvious for the vast majority of market practitioners, but economists have produced a myriad of results showing that investors cannot agree to disagree. One implication of "cannot agree to disagree" results is that differences in private information per se do not generate security transactions, since agents learn from observing security prices that adjust to reflect the information of all parties. Arrow (1986) appropriately calls this implication "[a conclusion] flatly contrary to observation."[2] Because they are not standard, I discuss in section 3 of this lecture some empirical evidence supporting these two central assumptions of the model.

Heterogeneous beliefs make possible the coexistence of optimists and pessimists in a market. The cost asymmetry between going long and going short on an asset implies that optimists' views are expressed more fully than pessimists' views in the market, and thus even when opinions are on average unbiased, prices are biased upwards. Finally, fluctuating beliefs give even the most optimistic the hope that, in the future, an even more optimistic buyer may appear. Thus a buyer would be willing to pay more than the discounted value she attributes to an asset's future payoffs, because the ownership of the asset gives her the option to resell the asset to a future optimist.

The difference between what a buyer is willing to pay and her valuation of the future payoffs of the asset—or equivalently, the value of the resale option—is identified as a bubble.[3] An increase in the volatility of beliefs increases the value of the resale option, thus increasing the divergence between asset prices and fundamental valuation, and also increases the volume of trade. Hence, in the model, bubble episodes are associated with increases in trading volume. As we argue in section 2.1, the connection between high trading volume and bubbles is a well-established, stylized fact. This relationship between bubbles and trading distinguishes models of bubbles based on heterogeneous beliefs and cost asymmetries from "rational bubble" theories.[4] A rational bubble is characterized by a continuous rise in an asset's price. Investors are content to hold the asset at the current price, because they believe that they are compensated for any risk of the bubble bursting by a suitable expected rate of price increase. In contrast to models based on heterogeneous beliefs and costly short-selling, rational bubble theories fail to explain the association between bubbles and high trading volume and cannot be invoked to explain bubbles in assets that have final payoffs at a maturity date T, such as many credit instruments.[5]

Market prices are determined at each point in time by the amount that the marginal buyer is willing to pay for the asset. When beliefs are not homogeneous, this marginal buyer is the least optimistic investor that is still a buyer of the asset. An increase in the capacity of individual investors to buy the asset, perhaps through increased leverage, allows for more extreme optimists to acquire the full supply of the asset at any point in time and thus increases the value of the resale option. When investors have limited capital and restricted access to leverage or limited capacity to bear risk, an increase in the supply of the asset is accompanied by a less optimistic marginal buyer. Thus the valuation that the marginal buyer has of future payoffs declines as supply increases, because the marginal buyer attributes a smaller fundamental value to the asset. However, a buyer also knows today that because of the larger supply that needs to be absorbed, future marginal buyers are likely to be relatively less optimistic and thus the value of the resale option also declines. Hence an increase in the supply of the asset that is unexpected by current holders of the asset diminishes the difference between the price and the fundamental valuation of the marginal buyer—that is, it diminishes the size of the bubble. In section 2.2 I argue that increases in asset supply helped implode some well-known bubbles.

Robert Shiller's rightly influential *Irrational Exuberance*[6] postulates that bubbles result from feedback mechanisms in prices that amplify some initial "precipitating factors."[7] The model in this lecture ignores the effect of this endogenous price dynamic just as it ignores the learning from prices used by rational theorists to dismiss the possibility of disagreement. It does, however, depend on precipitating factors that would generate optimism at least among some investors. Asset price bubbles often coincide with (over)excitement about a recent real or fake innovation,[8] and for the purpose of this lecture one may think of "technological innovations," broadly construed, as the precipitating factors generating bubbles.

This lecture is organized as follows: In section 1, I summarize some relevant facts concerning the South Sea Bubble, one of the earliest well-documented occurrences of a bubble. In section 2, I present some evidence on the three stylized facts that inspire the model in this lecture—that asset price bubbles coincide with increases in trading volume, that asset price bubble deflation seems to match with increases in an asset's supply, and that asset price bubbles often occur in times of financial or technological innovation. In section 3,

I discuss some evidence for the assumption of costly short-selling and for the role of overconfidence in generating differences in beliefs. Section 4 presents an informal sketch of the model and a discussion of related issues such as the effect of leverage, the origin of optimism, and the role of corporations in sustaining bubbles. I summarize some empirical work that provides evidence for the model in section 5 and present some concluding thoughts in section 6. A formal model is exposited in the appendix.

1 AN EXAMPLE: THE SOUTH SEA BUBBLE

One of the earliest well-documented occurrences of a bubble was the extraordinary rise and fall of the prices of shares of the South Sea Company and other similar joint-stock companies in Great Britain in 1720. At its origins in 1710, the South Sea Company had been granted a monopoly to trade with Spain's South American colonies. However, during most of the early eighteenth century Great Britain was at war with Spain's Philip V and the South Sea Company never did much goods-trading with South America, although it did achieve limited success as a slave trader. The real business of the South Sea Company was to exchange its stock for British government debt. The new equity owners would receive a liquid share with the right to perpetual annual interest payments in exchange for government debt, which paid a higher interest rate but was difficult to trade. In the first months of 1720, the Company and its rival, the Bank of England, engaged in a competition for the right to acquire the debt of the British government. After deliberating for more than two months, the House of Commons passed a bill favoring the South Sea Company. The bill was then "hurried through all its stages with unexampled rapidity"[9] and received royal assent on the same day, April 7, 1720, that it passed the House of Lords. The stock of the company that had traded for £120 in early January was now worth more than £300. However, this was just the beginning, and share prices approached £1,000 that summer.[10]

In *Famous First Bubbles*, Peter Garber argues that the prices attained by the South Sea Company shares in the summer of 1720 were justified by the belief in "[John] Law's prediction of a commercial expansion associated with the accumulation of a fund of credit."[11] Garber's monograph deals mostly with the Dutch Tulipmania, and Garber presents no original calculations on the South Sea Bubble, but cites Scott (1910–1912), who wrote, "[The] investor who in 1720 bought stock at 300 or even 400, may have been unduly optimistic, but there was still a possibility that his confidence would be rewarded in the future" (pages 313–314). Scott is commenting on prices of shares of the South Sea Company that prevailed until May 18th, before share prices doubled in a fortnight and continued to go up. In fact, in a passage a few pages later, Scott writes that by August 11 "unless the price of the stock in future issues had been set far above 1,000, the market quotations were unjustifiable ... Further, it would have been impossible to have floated the surplus stock at 1,000, much less at an increased issue price. This must have been apparent to anyone, who considered the position calmly."[12] This seems hardly an endorsement of the view that "[The

South Sea] episode is readily understandable as a case of speculators working on the basis of the best economic analysis available and pushing prices along with their changing view of market fundamentals."[13]

The South Sea Bubble involved much more than the company that names it. Other chartered companies holding British government debt such as the Bank of England and the East India Company also experienced rapid share-price appreciation, albeit in a less dramatic form than the South Sea Company. In addition, numerous other joint-stock companies, nicknamed "bubble companies," were founded. Mackay's (1932) catalog of bubble companies that were declared illegal by the "Bubble Act" of July 1720 is often quoted, but Mackay published his book in 1848, more than 120 years after the fact. However, a similar enumeration of bubble companies appeared earlier in Anderson (1787), pages 104–112.[14] Anderson's list gives a definite impression that many, though certainly not all, bubble schemes were fraudulent.

The speculation mechanism that we propose in this lecture was well understood by contemporary observers of the South Sea Bubble. The pioneering French-Irish economist Richard Cantillon, who was also a successful banker and merchant, wrote to Lady Mary Herbert on April 29, 1720, when shares of the South Sea Company reached £400, "People are madder than ever to run into the [South Sea Company] stock and don't so much as pretend to go in to remain in the stock but sell out again to profit."[15] Similarly, in his monumental history of British commerce, Anderson (1787) commented on the initial buyers of bubble companies' stocks:

"Yet many of those very subscribers were far from believing those projects feasible: it was enough for their purpose that there would very soon be a premium on the receipts for those subscriptions; when they generally got rid of them in the crowded alley to others more credulous than themselves."[16]

By offering to replace illiquid British national debt by liquid shares, the Lord Treasurer Robert Harley and the other founders of the South Sea Company were pioneers of a "business model" that created value by allowing investors to exercise the option to resell to a future optimist.

2 THREE STYLIZED FACTS

In this section, I present some evidence on three stylized facts that inspire my modeling choices: (i) asset price bubbles coincide with increases in trading volume; (ii) asset price bubble implosions seem to coincide with increases in an asset's supply; and (iii) asset price bubbles often coincide with financial or technological innovation. The evidence presented here is not meant to replace systematic empirical analysis, some of which we will discuss later, but simply to motivate the modeling that follows. To bring these stylized facts into focus, I will make references to aspects of four remarkable historical episodes of financial bubbles: the South Sea Bubble, the extraordinary rise of stock prices during the roaring twenties, the Internet bubble, and the recent credit bubble. I have already provided a short description of the South Sea Bubble and will assume that readers are familiar with a basic outline of the latter three episodes.

2.1 BUBBLES AND TRADING VOLUME

Carlos et al. (2006) document that trading on Bank of England stock rose from 2,000 transactions per year from 1717 to 1719 to 6,846 transactions in the bubble year of 1720. They also estimate that 150% of the outstanding stocks of the East India Company and of the Royal African Company turned over in 1720.

Accounts of the stock market boom of 1928–1929 also emphasize overtrading. In fact, the annual turnover (value of shares traded as a percentage of the value of outstanding shares) at NYSE climbed from 100% per annum during the years 1925 to 1927 to over 140% in 1928 and 1929.[17] Daily share-trading volume reached new all-time records ten times in 1928 and three times in 1929. No similar trading-volume record was set for nearly forty years, until April 1, 1968, when President Johnson announced he would not seek re-election.[18]

At the peak of the dotcom bubble, Internet stocks had three times the turnover of similar non-dotcom stocks.[19] Lamont and Thaler (2003) studied six cases of spinoffs during that bubble—episodes when publicly traded companies did an equity carve-out by selling a fraction of a subsidiary to the market via an initial public offering (IPO), and announced a plan to spin off the remaining shares of the subsidiary to the parent-company shareholders. A well-known example was Palm and 3Com. Palm, which made hand-held personal organizers, was owned by 3Com, which produced network systems and services. On March 2, 2000, 3Com sold 5% of its stake in Palm via an IPO. 3Com also announced that it would deliver the remaining shares of Palm to 3Com shareholders before the end of that year. Lamont and Thaler document that prior to the spin-off, shares in these six carve-outs, including Palm, sold for substantially more than the value of the shares embedded in the original company's shares. Since shares of the parent company would necessarily sell for a non-negative price after the spin-off, the observed relationship between the price of carve-outs and original companies' shares indicates a violation of the law of one price, one of the fundamental postulates of textbook finance theory. In addition, the trading volume of the shares in the carve-outs was astonishing—the *daily* turnover in the six cases studied by Lamont and Thaler averaged 38%,[20] a signal that buyers of the carve-outs, just like the buyers of bubble companies' stocks in 1720, were looking for others more credulous than themselves.

It is frequently argued that excessive trading causes asset prices to exceed fundamental valuations. We will not be making that argument here. In our model, excessive trading and prices that exceed fundamentals have a common cause. However, the often-observed correlation between asset-price bubbles and high trading volume is one of the most intriguing pieces of empirical evidence concerning bubbles and must be accounted in any theoretical attempt to understand these speculative episodes.

2.2 BUBBLES' IMPLOSION AND INCREASES IN ASSET SUPPLY

The South Sea Bubble lasted less than a year, but in that short period there was a huge increase in the supply of joint-stock company shares. New issues doubled the amount of shares outstanding of the South Sea Company and more than tripled those of the Royal African Company. Numerous other joint-stock companies were started during that year. The directors of the South Sea Company seem to have understood that the increase in the supply of shares of joint-stock companies threatened their own capacity to sell stock at inflated prices. Harris (1994) thoroughly examined the wording of the Bubble Act of 1720, in which Parliament banned joint-stock companies not authorized by Royal Charter or the extension of corporate charters into new ventures, and the historical evidence on interests and discourses, and concluded that "the [Bubble Act] was a special-interest legislation for the [South Sea Company], which controlled its framing and its passage." In any case, the South Sea Company directors used the Bubble Act to sue old chartered companies that had moved into "financial" activities and were competing with the South Sea Company for speculators' capital.

As the dotcom bubble inflated, there were numerous IPOs, but in each of these only a fraction of the shares were effectively sold. The remaining shares were assigned to insiders, venture capital funds, institutions, and sophisticated investors, who had agreements to hold their shares for a "lockup" period, often 6 months. An extraordinary number of lockup expirations for dotcom companies occurred during the first half of 2000, vastly increasing the supply of shares.[21] Venture capital firms that had distributed $3.9 billion to limited partners in the third quarter of 1999, distributed $21 billion during the first quarter of 2000, either by giving the newly unlocked shares to the limited partners or by selling these shares and distributing cash.[22] The bursting of the bubble in early 2000 coincided with this dramatic increase in the *float* (total number of shares available to the public) of firms in the Internet sector.

The recent credit bubble was characterized by an inordinate demand for liquid "safe assets," usually displaying a AAA rating from one or more of the major credit rating agencies. Financial engineering and rosy assumptions concerning housing price growth and correlations of defaults allowed issuers to transform a large fraction of subprime mortgages[23] into AAA credit. Subprime mortgage loans were pooled to serve as collateral for a mortgage-backed security (MBS), a collection of securities (tranches) that may have different priorities on the cash flows generated by the collateral. The senior tranche typically received a AAA rating. Lower-rated tranches of MBSs in turn could be pooled as collateral for a credit default obligation (CDO). The senior tranches of the CDO would again have a AAA rating. Lower-rated tranches of CDOs could then be combined to serve as collateral for the tranches of a CDO-squared, and lower-rated tranches of a CDO-squared could be combined with other securities to serve as collateral for the tranches of a CDO-cubed, and so on.

The high prices commanded by the instruments resulting from this securitization process increased the demand by issuers for residential mortgage loans and lowered the cost of taking a mortgage, thus facilitating housing purchases. In 2000, issues of private-label mortgage-backed securities (PLS)—that is, mortgage-backed securities that were not issued by government-sponsored enterprises (GSEs)—financed $572 billion in U.S. residential mortgages. By the end of 2006, the volume of outstanding mortgages financed by PLSs had reached $2.6 trillion. Many of these PLSs used less-than-prime mortgage loans, and the combined annual subprime and Alt-A origination grew from an estimated $171 billion in 2002 to $877 billion in 2005, an annualized growth rate of 72%.[24]

Several developments added dramatically to the effective supply of securities backed by housing-related assets. In the summer of 2005, the International Swaps and Derivatives Association (ISDA) created a standardized credit default swap (CDS), or insurance against default, for mortgage-backed securities. A CDS is a contract in which a buyer, or *long* party, makes regular payments to a seller, or *short* party, in exchange for a promise by the seller to insure the buyer against losses in certain adverse credit events such as defaults. These contracts allowed a pessimist to buy insurance on a subprime MBS he did not own. Early in 2006, Markit launched ABX.HE, subprime mortgage-backed credit derivative indexes. Each ABX index was based on 20 MBSs with the same credit rating and issued within a six-month window. The level of the index reflected the price at which a CDS on this set of MBSs was trading. Investors who had optimistic views concerning the risks in subprime MBS could now acquire a short position in a AAA series of the ABX index. If the market became more positive about these securities in the future, the cost of the corresponding CDS would drop and the shorts would make a profit. In the summer of 2006, ISDA went further and created a standard CDS contract on CDO tranches, allowing investors who had a pessimistic view of, say, AAA tranches of subprimes to effectively take short exposures to the subprime market—a market in which, for institutional reasons, it was often difficult to short individual securities. In this way, the supply of AAA tranches of CDOs was effectively increased.

None of these developments, however, were fully adequate to satisfy the demand for AAA paper by institutions that, often for regulatory reasons, found it necessary to buy highly rated securities. Synthetic CDOs were a perfect supply response to this demand. These were CDOs that did not contain any actual MBSs but instead consisted of a portfolio of short positions on CDSs and some high-quality liquid assets. The buyer of a (funded) tranche of a synthetic CDO was entitled to interest payments partly funded by CDS premia on a set of reference securities. Defaults on the reference securities triggered write-downs of principal. The rating agencies rated the senior tranches of these synthetic CDOs as AAA. The creation of a standard CDS for MBSs, and the consequent increase in supply of these insurance contracts, allowed Goldman Sachs, Deutsche Bank, and other Wall Street powerhouses, but also smaller firms such as Tricardia, to create an enormous supply of synthetic CDOs. Wall Street could now satisfy the demands of a German Landesbank for additional U.S. AAA mortgage bonds without any new houses being built in Arizona.[25] The associated increase in the supply of assets carrying housing risk seems to have been enough to satisfy not only optimistic German Landesbanks but also every Lehman trader or Citi SIV portfolio manager who wanted to hold housing risk. In this way, the implosion of the credit bubble parallels the implosion of the South Sea and dotcom bubbles.[26]

2.3 ASSET PRICE BUBBLES AND THE ARRIVAL OF "NEW TECHNOLOGIES"

Asset price bubbles tend to appear in periods of excitement about innovations. The stock market bubble of the 1920s was driven primarily by the new technology stocks of the time, namely the automobile, aircraft, motion picture, and radio industries; the dotcom bubble has an obvious connection to Internet technology. In the United States there has been notable attention to the recent housing bubble. However the housing bubble was simply one manifestation of an enormous credit bubble that took place in the early part of this century. In April 2006, while the Case-Shiller housing index reached its peak, you could buy a 5-year CDS on Greek debt for less than 15 bp (.15%) per year.[27] Similarly, in April 2006, the average spread for a CDS on debt from Argentina, a country that had defaulted repeatedly and as recently as 2002, was less than 3% per year.

This credit bubble coincided with advances in financial engineering, the introduction of new financial instruments and hedging techniques, and advances in risk measurement that promised better risk management and "justified" lower risk premia.

3 EVIDENCE FOR COSTLY SHORT-SELLING AND OVERCONFIDENCE

Economists typically treat short sales of an asset as the purchase of a negative amount of that asset, and assume that short sales generate just as much transaction cost as purchases. Although there are exceptions—such as future markets—legal and institutional constraints make this assumption problematic in almost all cases. To short an asset requires finding a lender for that asset and, because often there are no organized markets for borrowing an asset, finding a lender can be difficult. In addition, securities are often loaned on call, and borrowers face the risk of replacing the borrowed securities or being forced to cover their short position.[28] Securities loans are often collateralized with cash. The security lender pays interest on the collateral, but the lender pays the borrower of the security a rebate rate that is less than the market rate for cash funds. Rebate rates may be negative and thus the fee effectively paid by the borrower of the security can exceed market interest rates. Among other factors, the rebate rate reflects the supply and demand for a particular security's loan and the likelihood that the lender recalls the security. D'Avolio (2002) documents that rebate rates are negatively correlated while recalls are positively correlated with measures of divergence of opinions. The possibility of recall makes shorting securities with a small float and/or little liquidity especially risky. Individual MBS securities or certain tranches of CDOs had relatively small face values.

Diether et al. (2002) provide evidence that stocks with higher dispersion in analysts' earnings forecasts earn lower future returns than otherwise similar stocks. It is reasonable to take the dispersion in analysts' forecasts as a proxy for differences in opinion about a stock, and the observation of lower returns for stocks with more difference in opinions is consistent with the hypothesis that prices will reflect a relatively optimistic view whenever going long is cheaper than going short. In contrast, the evidence reported by Diether et al. (2002) is inconsistent with a view that dispersion in analysts' forecasts proxies for risk, since in this case stocks with higher dispersion should not exhibit lower returns.

There are of course many possible ways in which differences in beliefs may arise. In this lecture I will assume that differences in beliefs are related to overconfidence—the tendency of individuals to exaggerate the precision of their knowledge. The original paper documenting overconfidence is Alpert and Raiffa (1982). Overconfidence has been documented in a variety of groups of decision-makers, including engineers (Kidd (1970)) and entrepreneurs (Cooper et al. (1988)). Tetlock (2005) discusses overconfidence in a group of professional experts who earn a living commenting or advising on political and economic trends, such as journalists, foreign policy specialists, economists and intelligence analysts. The vast majority of these pundits' predictions seem to do no better than random chance.

Even more directly relevant to the topic of this lecture is the paper by Ben-David et al. (2010). Between June 2001 and September 2010, Duke University collected quarterly surveys of senior finance executives, the majority of whom were CFOs and financial vice-presidents. Among other questions, the respondents were asked to report a number they believed had a one-in-ten chance of falling above the actual S&P return over the next year. The respondents were also asked to report a number they believed had a one-in-ten chance of falling below the actual S&P return over the next year. These two numbers form the 10–90 interval—that is, the interval of numbers for which a respondent believes there is a 10% chance that the actual S&P returns would fall to the left of that interval and a 10% chance that the actual returns would fall to the right of that interval. The 10–90 interval should cover 80% of the realizations. In total, the surveys collected over 12,500 of these intervals and the realized returns in the S&P over each year following a survey fell within the executives' 10–90 intervals only 33% of the time. Evidently, these senior finance executives grossly overestimated the precision of their knowledge concerning future stock returns.

4 SKETCH OF A MODEL

The appendix contains a model connecting difference of opinions and costly shorting to speculation and trading. The model in the appendix is a simplified version of an already stylized model developed in Scheinkman and Xiong (2003), who were inspired by a pioneering paper by Harrison and Kreps (1978). Harrison and Kreps were the first to formally show that short-sale constraints and heterogeneous beliefs imply that buyers of an asset may be willing to pay a price that exceeds their own valuation of the future dividends of that asset.[29]

In the model in the appendix, there are two types of investors that for simplicity are assumed to be risk-neutral. Thus, if forced to hold an asset until maturity, these investors are willing to pay for that asset a price that equals the asset's expected payoff discounted at the risk-free rate. Differences of opinions arise because investors estimate future payoffs of a risky asset using signals they believe are useful to predict payoffs. Some investors are "rational" and use signals in an optimal fashion. Others attribute value to information they should ignore—perhaps a cable-TV host named J.C. recommending a "buy" or a "sell." In the model, "irrational" investors are right on average, but depending on the particular value of the useless information that they observe, they can be excessively optimistic or excessively pessimistic.[30] Thus, on average, opinions of investors are unbiased. I also assume for simplicity that short sales are not allowed, although it would suffice to assume costly short-selling.

Suppose that an asset will have a payoff two years from now which may be high or low with equal probability. Suppose further that one year from now, J.C. may voice an opinion on which of the two payoffs is likely to occur. The TV host's opinion is totally unfounded, but there is a large group of investors that believe that J.C.'s views are valuable. Since there are no short sales allowed, if each group of agents has more than enough capital to acquire the whole float of the asset at their own valuation, then once J.C.'s opinion is known, members of the most optimistic group would acquire the whole supply and, because they compete with others of the same group, buyers would end up paying their expected payoff. If J.C. claims the higher payoff is likely to obtain, the irrational agents would pay a price that reflects an optimistic view of the asset payoff. If J.C. claims the lower payoff is likely to occur, then the irrational agents would be pessimists, but rational agents would still be willing to buy the asset paying a price equal to the rational-agents' expected payoff.

And if J. C. is silent, both agents agree that the asset is worth the rational-agents' expected payoff. Now suppose a market where the asset is traded opens today. A rational investor knows that if a year from now J. C. screams "high dividend," she would have the option to sell the asset at that moment to an irrational investor at a price higher than her own valuation would be at that point. Otherwise, if J. C. stays silent or utters a pessimistic opinion, the investor would be happy to hold the asset. Thus a rational buyer would be willing to pay today in excess of her own valuation of future payoffs, because she acquires an option to resell the asset one year from now if J. C. screams "high dividend." The more likely it is that in one year from now J. C. would claim that a high dividend will obtain, the larger would be the amount that a rational investor would pay for the asset today. Because of the symmetry we assumed between the probability that J. C. claims that a high payoff will occur and the probability that J. C. claims that a low payoff will occur, the rational investor would pay more for the resale option when there is a higher probability that J. C. would emit any opinion. Similarly, an irrational investor would pay more than his own valuation for the asset today, because he knows that if J. C. claims next year that a low payoff will occur, he would be able to sell the asset to someone that he would judge to be over optimistic.

In the context of the model, I define a bubble as the value that a buyer pays for the option to resell. Thus a bubble occurs when a buyer pays in excess of her valuation of future dividends, because she values the opportunity to resell to a more optimistic buyer in the future. Since buyers would tend to be among the most optimistic agents, it would be natural to call the difference between buyer's valuation and a "rational" valuation also a bubble. Here, I do not include buyers' excessive optimism as part of the bubble, and thus the definition of a bubble used in this lecture is somewhat conservative. Although bubbles certainly coincide with periods in which excessive optimism prevails among many investors, the definition of a bubble used here emphasizes the role of the existence of *divergent* opinions as opposed to the actual opinions held by asset owners during these episodes.

If the asset is held initially by rational and irrational agents, trades will occur whenever J. C. emits an opinion. On average we would get a higher volume of trade whenever there is a larger probability that J. C. would give an opinion. Thus the same cause—the frequency of J. C. opinions—creates differences in opinion, a bubble, and trading. In the appendix we show that this difference in opinions can be identified with overconfidence.

The value of the resale option is naturally a function of the costs of funds. The higher the interest rate faced by investors, the less they are willing to pay for the resale option. The model in the appendix thus gives a simple theoretical justification for the argument that lower interest rates are conducive to bubbles. In the case of multiple trading periods, shorter horizons yield fewer opportunities to resell, making the resale option less valuable.

The model in this lecture ignores two forces that have been invoked to dismiss the importance of differences in beliefs. The first is learning—the irrational agents should eventually learn that the signal they are using is useless. Learning no doubt plays a role in diminishing differences in beliefs over long horizons, but bubbles last for a relatively short period when learning must have a limited effect. The second argument brought against the importance of irrational beliefs is survivorship. As argued by Friedman (1966), irrational agents should lose wealth on average and thus have a vanishing influence on market outcomes. However, Yan (2008) performed calibration exercises on Friedman's argument and concluded that for reasonable parameter values, it may take *hundreds of years* for irrational investors to lose even half their wealth. Because bubbles are relatively short-lived, I will ignore learning and survivorship and emphasize other forces that create and deflate bubbles.

4.1 LIMITED CAPITAL

If irrational investors have limited access to capital and the supply of the asset increases, perhaps as a result of sales by insiders, then even when J.C. emits an optimistic opinion, irrational investors may not be able to buy the full asset float while paying their own valuation. When the capital constraint of irrational investors is severe enough, even when irrational optimism occurs, the marginal buyer may be a rational investor who has a lower valuation of the asset. Hence when irrational agents have limited capital, the size of the bubble depends on the asset supply. For the same reason, if the asset's float is large enough, some of the asset supply may end up in the hands of rational investors even though irrational investors are optimists and have a higher valuation for the asset. As a consequence, the turnover (volume traded as a fraction of the float) of an asset is smaller for assets with a larger float.

In the model developed in the appendix, in the presence of capital constraints, an increase in supply that is not fully expected leads to a deflation of the bubble. This was one of the main insights in Hong et al. (2006). In the Internet bubble, increases in supply were often the result of sales by insiders. Hong et al. (2006) observed that it is reasonable to assume that unexpected sales by insiders lead to a revision of forecasts by current investors and potential buyers and that this revision in beliefs must reinforce the tendency of supply increases to produce bubbles' implosion.

4.2 LEVERAGE

The model in the appendix does not explicitly treat leverage, but the observations on limited capital also provide insights on the role of leverage. Investors can often access capital using their purchases of assets as collateral for loans. The amount loaned to finance the purchase of one unit of a risky asset would typically be less than the price of the asset. The difference between the price of the asset and the value of the loan is the *margin* and its reciprocal the *leverage*. A homeowner that acquired a house in 2004 with a 5% down payment would thus have a leverage of 20. Higher leverage would increase the access to capital by optimists and thus help to augment and sustain bubbles.

In the presence of belief disagreements, pessimists should be willing to make loans collateralized by the risky asset to optimists. Market conditions determine the leverage and interest rates charged on these loans, but one should expect that pessimists would demand relatively low leverage and/

or high interest rates. Pioneered by Geanokoplos,[31] a literature which studies the equilibrium determination of leverage and interest rates for loans from pessimists to optimists has developed.

In reality however, because of tax or regulatory reasons, not all optimists are adequate holders of certain risky assets. For instance, homeowners benefit from the absence of taxation on imputed rent and the unique treatment of capital gains in owner-occupied homes. Although they were not the most appropriate direct investors in houses, optimistic banks had another way to benefit from the housing price increases that they anticipated in 2004. They could make loans charging more than prime rates to subprime buyers that the banks believed would be capable of repaying their loans in the very likely event that house prices continued to behave as they had in the previous ten years. Contemporary analysts' reports from major financial institutions recognized the potentially negative impact of house-price decline on the value of mortgage-related securities, but underestimated the probability of occurrence of these adverse events. Thus, as argued by Foote et al. (2012), it is reasonable to conclude that some investors in mortgage-related securities were simply excessively optimistic about the possibility of house-price declines.[32] Money market funds, which by their nature must invest in short-term "safe" securities, participate heavily in repo markets—essentially loans collateralized by securities. A money market fund that was willing to finance 98.4% of the purchase price of a AAA mortgage security to an investor in 2006 probably thought that these securities were actually nearly risk-free, warranting a leverage of 60. In this way, a chain of optimists provided leverage to optimistic investors in the housing market.[33] This chain was reinforced by U.S. regulation that placed low capital-risk weights on securities deemed AAA by "Nationally Recognized Statistical Rating Organizations" and by similar regulations in other countries, and was amplified by innovations in finance, such as the MBS based CDO. It is ironic that this same process of innovation in financial engineering eventually allowed pessimists to express their negative views on these markets and speeded up the implosion of the bubble.

Compared to pessimists, optimists without direct access to a risky asset are bound to accept terms more favorable to the borrower on loans backed by that asset. Thus it is reasonable to argue that during the credit bubble, leverage from optimists was a more important source of capital for mortgage-securities investors than leverage from pessimists.

4.3 ORIGINS OF OPTIMISM

The formal model exposited in the appendix is silent concerning the precipitating factors that generate optimism among investors. In practice, investors rely on advice from friends, acquaintances, and "experts." Some advice is without doubt biased because of the financial incentives faced by experts, but it has been documented that during speculative episodes, apparently unbiased advisors also issue overoptimistic forecasts.[34]

Motivated by the coincidence of bubbles and periods of excitement about new technologies, Hong et al. (2008) proposed a theory based on the role of formal or informal advisors. In the model in Hong et al. (2008), there are two types of advisors. Tech-savvy advisors understand the new technologies—think of a finance quant during the credit bubble—while old fogeys are uniformly pessimistic concerning the new technologies. Tech-savvies may be well-intentioned advisors, but worry about being confused with old fogeys. As does the art critic in Tom Wolfe's *The Painted Word*, tech-savvies worry that "to be against what is new is not to be modern. Not to be modern is to write yourself out of the scene. Not to be in the scene is to be nowhere."[35]

To ensure that their advisees do not confuse them with old fogeys, tech-savvies issue overly optimistic forecasts concerning assets related to the new technologies. Rational investors understand the advisors' motivations and "de-bias" the advice, but naïve investors take advisors' recommendations at face value. Although the presence of old fogeys tends to depress prices of the assets related to the new technology, when there is a sufficient number of naïve investors guided by tech-savvies, the biased advice overcomes the effect of old fogeys and induces over-optimism among investors.

4.4 EXECUTIVE COMPENSATION, RISK-TAKING, AND SPECULATION

Although our discussion until now has been mainly concerned with the behavior of individual investors, corporations have played a central role in recent bubbles. The implosion of the credit bubble and consequent Wall Street bailout brought deserved attention to the risk-taking behavior of financial firms during that episode and led to calls for compensation reforms that would eliminate excessive incentives for managers to take risks.

The standard economists' approach to compensation uses the "Principal-Agent" framework, which emphasizes how managerial contracts are set by boards as shareholders' representatives to solve the misalignment of interests between managers and stockholders. Bebchuk and Fried (2006) and other critics of this approach contend that CEOs have been able essentially to set their own contracts through captured boards and remuneration committees, and that major reforms in corporate governance to increase shareholder power are necessary to remediate the current state of affairs.

The critics of the standard approach to compensation are no doubt correct in pointing out important ways in which the selection of board members and executive pay negotiations depart from the idealized "arms-length" bargaining of the principal-agent paradigm. However, the critics have more difficulties explaining how the relatively recent phenomenon of rise in pay and stock-based compensation has coincided with the dramatic rise in shareholder influence that began in the 1980s.[36] In fact, we have observed a tendency towards greater board independence, a higher proportion of externally recruited CEOs, a decrease in the average tenure of CEOs, and higher forced CEO turnover during this period.

Bolton et al. (2006) point out that a speculative market creates a divergence between the interests of short-term versus long-term stockholders and between the interests of current versus future stockholders. Short-term stockholders would like managers to take actions that increase the

speculative value of shares, even if at the cost of the fundamental value of the firm. If stockholders with a short-term
horizon dominate a board, they would select contracts for
managers that emphasize stock price-based compensation
that vests early, to align the interests of managers with their
own interests.[37]

Examining a panel of U.S. financial firms during the
period of 1992–2008, Cheng et al. (2010) found substantial
cross-firm differences in total executive compensation even
after controlling for firm size. Top management level of pay
is positively correlated with price-based risk-taking measures
including firm beta, return volatility, the sensitivity of firm
stock price to the ABX subprime index, and tail cumulative
return performance. Managers' compensation and firm risk-
taking are not related to governance variables but co-vary
with ownership by institutional investors who tend to have
short-termist preferences and the power to influence a firm's
management policy.[38]

The empirical results in Cheng et al. (2010) indicate that
governance reforms are hardly the solution for excessive risk-
taking by financial firms.

5 SOME ADDITIONAL EVIDENCE

Two data sets, both coincidentally from China, provide
additional evidence to support the mechanisms I have
proposed in this lecture. These data sets have been used
in research that was motivated by the bubble models discussed in this lecture.

Between 1993 and 2000, 73 Chinese firms offered two classes of shares, A and B, with identical rights. Until 2001, domestic Chinese investors could buy only A shares while foreign investors could hold only B shares. Mei et al. (2009) used these data to test implications of models of heterogeneous beliefs and short-sale constraints. This is particularly appropriate, because at that time Chinese buyers of A shares faced very stringent short-sale constraints, and IPOs and SEOs (Seasoned Equity Offerings) were tightly controlled by the central government. Despite their identical rights to dividends and voting rights, A shares traded on average at a premium of 420% relative to B shares. The annual turnover of B shares, around 100%, was similar to the turnover of NYSE shares at the time, while A shares traded at 500% a year. The relatively large panel of 73 stocks allows Mei et al. (2009) to control for cross-sectional differences in risk and liquidity and time variations in China's risk and risk-premium. They find that A-share turnover is significantly positively correlated with the A-B share premium, and in fact 20% of that premium can be "explained" by turnover variation. On the other hand, B-share turnover had a positive association with the A-B premium, albeit not statistically significant. This supports the hypothesis that A-share prices (but not B-share prices) were driven by speculation. Mei et al. (2009) also show that the A-B share premium and A-share turnover increase with a firm's idiosyncratic return volatility, a proxy for uncertainty. This is consistent with the bubble theory based on heterogeneous beliefs if one believes that more fundamental uncertainty would increase fluctuations in differences in beliefs.

Furthermore, Mei et al. (2009) show that controlling for the proportion of days in which a share did not display a price change—a proxy for liquidity that has been used in the finance literature—does not significantly change the association between A-share turnover and the A-B premium. To determine whether trading in A and B shares was driven by speculation or liquidity, they examined the cross-sectional correlation between share turnover and asset float of A and B shares. Liquidity typically increases with asset float, since as float increases, it is easier for buyers to match up with sellers. On the other hand, as we argued above, in the presence of speculation and limited capital, a larger float is associated with a smaller turnover. Mei et al. (2009) find a significant negative relationship between share turnover and float in A-share markets in 1993–2000, suggesting that the large trading volume in A shares was not a result of liquidity. However for B shares, which were held by more sophisticated foreign investors, Mei et al. (2009) found that turnover was positively associated with float—suggesting that liquidity played a role in attracting trading in B shares.

On February 28, 2001, the Chinese government allowed domestic investors to buy B shares provided they used foreign currency. The A-B premium decreased but almost exclusively because B-share prices went up. Monthly B-share turnover in the six months following this event averaged 44%, almost four times the monthly turnover of these shares in the six months preceding the liberalization. Moreover, the coefficient of the A-B premium on B-share turnover becomes significantly negative after the liberalization. This contrasts with the results for the earlier period (positive and insignificant) and indicates that speculation became a relevant component of B-share price formation. In addition, after Chinese investors were allowed to buy B shares using foreign currency, the coefficient of a regression of turnover of B shares on B-share float turned from positive to negative, suggesting again that trading in B shares may have become more driven by speculation.

The Chinese warrant bubble of 2005–2008 was used by Xiong and Yu (2011) to test predictions of heterogeneous beliefs-cum-short-sale constraints theories of bubbles. From 2005 to 2008, eighteen Chinese companies issued put warrants on their stock with maturities ranging from six months to two years. These warrants gave the holder the right to sell the issuing companies' stocks at predetermined prices during a period.

The extraordinary rise of prices in Chinese stocks between 2005 and 2007 made it almost certain that these warrants would expire without being exercised. In fact, using the familiar Black-Scholes option-pricing formula, Xiong and Yu (2011) calculated that close to their expiration date, these warrants often were worth less than .05 hundredths of a yuan. However, prices of these virtually worthless warrants varied substantially and averaged .948 yuan during the days in which their Black-Scholes values fell below .05 hundredths of a yuan. Xiong and Yu (2011) also provide other bounds on the value of warrants that are violated in this sample of warrants.

One security Xiong and Yu (2011) describe in detail is the put warrant on the stock of WuLiangYe Corporation, a liquor producer.[39] The put warrant was issued on April 3, 2006, in-the-money with an exercise price of 7.95 yuan while WuLiangYe's stock traded at 7.11 yuan. Initially, the warrant was valued close to 1 yuan, but in two weeks, WuLiangYe's stock price exceeded the strike and the warrant never returned in-the-money. On October 15, 2007, the stock reached a peak of 71.56 yuan and then drifted down to close at 26 yuan at the expiration of the warrant on April 2, 2008. The calculation by Xiong and Yu (2011) is that from July 2007, the Black-Scholes price of this put was below .05 hundredths of a yuan, but the warrant traded for a few yuans, and only dropped below its initial price of .99 yuan in the last few trading days.

As in other episodes discussed in this lecture, these unjustifiably high prices were accompanied by trading frenzies. The warrants with a Black-Scholes value of less than .05 hundredths of a yuan had an average daily turnover rate of 328%. On their last trading day, when they were all virtually worthless, these 18 warrants, on average, turned over 100% of their float every 20 minutes! The trading volume on the warrant on the stock of WuLiangYe Corporation reached 1,841% of that warrant's float in the last trading day. Xiong and Yu (2011) show that as predicted by the models discussed here, the size of the price bubble on a warrant was positively correlated with the trading volume of that warrant or the time remaining to expiration, and negatively correlated with the warrant's float.

6 SOME FINAL OBSERVATIONS

One of the questions left unanswered in this lecture is whether one could use the signals associated with bubbles, such as inordinate trading volume or high leverage, to detect and perhaps stop bubbles. One of the difficulties in using these signals is that we know next to nothing about false positives. For instance, the typical empirical paper studying the association between volume of trade and bubbles examines data during a bubble episode.

Even if we could effectively detect bubbles, it is not obvious that we should try to stop all types of bubbles. Although credit bubbles have proven to have devastating consequences, the relationship between bubbles and technological innovation suggests that some of these episodes may play a positive role in economic growth. The increase in the price of assets during a bubble makes it easier to finance investments related to the new technologies.

The most straightforward policy recommendations that arise from the arguments advanced in this lecture is that to avoid bubbles, policy makers should consider limiting leverage and facilitating, instead of impeding, short-selling. In the panic that followed the implosion of the credit bubble, the SEC banned short sales of financial stocks. In August 2011, as the markets questioned the health and funding needs of European financial institutions, France, Italy, Spain and Belgium imposed bans on short sales of financial stocks. Each of these interventions may have given a temporary respite to the markets for these assets, but caused losses to investors that were short these assets and had to cover their positions. Investors learned one more time that it is dangerous to bet against overvalued assets—a lesson that they will surely keep in mind in the next bubble.

APPENDIX: A FORMAL MODEL

A.1 THE BASIC MODEL

I first exposit a simple model to illustrate the role of costly shorting and differences in beliefs in generating bubbles and the association between bubbles and trading. Consider four periods $t = 1, 2, 3, 4$; a single good; and a single risky asset in finite supply S. In addition to the risky asset, there also exists a risk-free technology. An investment of $\delta \leq 1$ units of the good in the risk-free technology at t yields one unit in period $t + 1$. Assume there are a large number of risk-neutral investors that only value consumption in the final period $t = 4$. Each investor is endowed with an amount W_0 of the good.

The risky asset produces dividends at times $t = 2, 3, 4$. At each $t = 2, 3, 4$ each unit of the risky asset pays a dividend $\theta_t \in \{\theta_l, \theta_h\}$ with $\theta_h > \theta_l$. In what follows, I will refer to θ_h (θ_l) as the high (resp. low) dividend. Dividends at any t are independent of past and future dividends.[1] The probability that $\theta_t = \theta_l$ is .5, and we write

$$\bar{\theta} = E(\theta_t) = .5\theta_l + .5\theta_h.$$

Assets are traded at $t = 1, 2, 3, 4$. If a dividend is paid in period t, trading occurs after the dividend is distributed—that is, the asset trades ex-dividend and the buyer of the asset in period t has the rights to all dividends from time $t + 1$ on. Thus in the final period $t = 4$, the price of the asset $p_4 = 0$, since there are no dividends paid after period 4. The price at time $t = 1, 2, 3$ depends on the expectations of investors regarding the dividends to be paid in the future. We first calculate the willingness to pay of a "rational" risk-neutral investor that is not allowed to resell the asset after she buys it. Since the investor is risk-neutral, at time $t = 3$ she is willing to pay $\delta\bar{\theta}$ for a unit of the asset. In the absence of resale opportunities, at $t = 2$, the rational investor is willing to pay $\delta[\bar{\theta} + \delta\bar{\theta}] = (\delta + \delta^2)\bar{\theta}$. Finally, at $t = 1$ that same rational investor with no resale opportunities would be willing to pay

$$(\delta + \delta^2 + \delta^3)\bar{\theta}. \tag{1}$$

In addition, we suppose that at each $t = 1, 2, 3$, a signal s_t is observed after the dividend at t (if $t > 1$) is observed but before trading occurs at t. Each signal s_t assumes one of three values $\{0, 1, 2\}$, is independent of past realizations of the signal and of the dividends, and has no predictive power for future dividends. Thus the signal s_t is pure noise. There are, however, two sets of investors, A and B. Each set has many investors. Agents in group A are rational and understand that the distribution of future dividends is independent of s_t. Agents in B actually believe that s_t predicts θ_{t+1} and that the probability that $\theta_{t+1} = \theta_h$ given s_t is:

Probability $[\theta_{t+1} = \theta_h \,|\, s_t] = .5 + .25(s_t - 1)$.

Thus agents in group B believe that the probability of a high dividend at $t + 1$ increases with the observed s_t and that when $s_t = 0 (s_t = 2)$, $\theta_{t+1} = \theta_l$ (resp. $\theta_{t+1} = \theta_h$) is more probable. All agents agree that s_t does not help predict θ_{t+j} for $j \geq 2$, and thus the only disagreement among investors is whether

s_t can predict θ_{t+1}. To make agents in set B correct on average, and thus assure that *ex-ante* there are no optimistic or pessimistic investors, assume that the probability that $s_t = 0$ equals the probability that $s_t = 2$. Write $q < .5$ for this common probability, and observe that the probability that $s_t = 1$ is $1 - 2q > 0$.

In the case of binary random variables, forecasts have minimal precision[2] when the probability of each realization is $1/2$. This is exactly the forecast of rational agents here. Agents in group B, after observing $s_t = 1$, also have the same minimal forecast precision. However, if they observe $s_t = 0$ or $s_t = 2$ they employ forecasts that have higher precision, since they (mistakenly) believe that one of the two possible events has a probability of $3/4$. In this sense agents in group B have an exaggerated view of the precision of their beliefs.

At time $t = 3$, rational agents in group A are willing to bid up to $\delta\bar{\theta}$ for a unit of the asset. However, if $s_3 = 2$, agents in set B believe that the probability of a high dividend in period 4 is .75. Since these agents are risk-neutral and the risk-free technology transforms δ units at time 2 into 1 unit at time 3, when $s_3 = 2$ members of group B are willing to pay up to

$$\delta(.75\theta_h + .25\theta_l) = \delta\left[\bar{\theta} + .25(\theta_h - \theta_l)\right] > \delta\bar{\theta}.$$

I assume that there are no short sales. Section A.2 below treats the case when there is limited capital in the hands of a group of investors, but I will initially assume that W_0 is large enough so that each group of investors has sufficient aggregate wealth to acquire the full supply of the asset at their own valuation. Suppose $s_3 = 2$. Since there are many agents in group B, no short sales, and agents in group B have sufficient wealth to acquire the full supply at their valuation, all risky assets end up in the hand of some agents in group B and competition among agents of group B guarantees that when $s_3 = 2$ the price is

$$p_3(2) = \delta\left[\overline{\theta} + .25(\theta_h - \theta_l)\right].$$

If $s_3 = 1$, then all agents value the asset at $\delta\overline{\theta}$, and thus

$$p_3(1) = \delta\overline{\theta}.$$

If $s_3 = 0$, agents in set B are unduly pessimistic and the asset ends up in the hands of some rational agents that pay

$$p_3(0) = \delta\overline{\theta}.$$

Since the probability that $s_3 = 2$ is q, the price p_3 equals $\delta\overline{\theta}$ with probability $1 - q$ and equals $\delta[\overline{\theta} + .25(\theta_h - \theta_l)] > \delta\overline{\theta}$ with probability q. Hence, before s_3 is observed, all agents anticipate that the price of the asset in period 3 will on average equal

$$Ep_3 = \delta[\overline{\theta} + .25q(\theta_h - \theta_l)]. \qquad (2)$$

Every agent in group A and in group B expects the payoff of the asset in period 4 to be on average exactly $\overline{\theta}$, but the average price in period 3 exceeds the discounted value of this expected payoff, $\delta\overline{\theta}$, by

$$\delta[.25q(\theta_h - \theta_l)],$$

reflecting the fact that for each realization of the signal s_3 a member of the most optimistic group would acquire the asset.

When $s_3 = 0$ ($s_3 = 2$) agents in group A (resp. B) are the most optimistic and end up holding the total supply of the asset. When $s_3 = 1$ both groups are equally optimistic and any distribution of asset holdings across the two groups is compatible with equilibrium.

Although the price paid in period t sometimes reflects the excessively optimistic views of group B agents, our definition of a bubble—that is, a bubble occurs when buyers pay more than they think the future dividends are worth—implies that there is no bubble in period 3. As I will show next, this is not the case for any $t < 3$.

At time $t = 2$, if $s_2 = 2$, agents in set B assume that the probability of a high dividend θ_h in period 3 is .75. Since s_3 has not yet been observed, agents in set B forecast the price in period 3 to be on average Ep_3. Thus, when $s_2 = 2$ agents in group B are willing to pay

$$p_2(2) = \delta(\overline{\theta} + .25(\theta_h - \theta_l) + Ep_3). \tag{3}$$

Similarly, if $s_2 = 1$ ($s_2 = 0$) agents of both types (resp. agents of type A) are willing to pay

$$p_2(0) = p_2(1) = \delta(\overline{\theta} + Ep_3).$$

Hence, before s_2 is observed, agents anticipate an average price for the asset:

$$\begin{aligned} Ep_2 &= \delta(\overline{\theta} + .25q(\theta_h - \theta_l) + Ep_3) \\ &= (\delta + \delta^2)[\overline{\theta} + .25q(\theta_h - \theta_l)]. \end{aligned} \tag{4}$$

A buyer of the asset in period 2 acquires the right to dividends in periods 3 and 4. Before s_2 is observed, agents of both types agree that these dividends are worth (in period 2) exactly $(\delta + \delta^2)\overline{\theta}$. However, the average price in period 2 exceeds this fundamental value by

$$(\delta + \delta^2) \times .25q(\theta_h - \theta_l).$$

This difference is a consequence of (i) the fact that in period 2 for each realization of the signal s_2, the asset will be sold to the highest bidder, and (ii) any buyer of the asset in period 2 acquires the right to resell it in period 3 to a buyer that is more optimistic than she is. (i) is worth $\delta \times .25q(\theta_h - \theta_l)$, while the option to resell in period 3 (ii) is worth $\delta^2 \times .25q(\theta_h - \theta_l)$. Furthermore, even in the event $s_2 = 0$ when "rational" (group A) agents acquire the full supply of the risky asset, these agents pay

$$\delta(\overline{\theta} + Ep_3) = \delta\overline{\theta} + \delta^2[\overline{\theta} + .25q(\theta_h - \theta_l)]. \tag{5}$$

This value exceeds the fundamental value, since buyers of the asset in period 2 will benefit from the resale option in period 3. When $s_2 = 1$, holders of the asset (in group A or B) are also willing to pay this same amount. Whereas in period 3, prices exceed fundamentals only if group B agents are optimistic, in period 2, prices exceed fundamentals even when group B agents are unduly pessimistic.

More importantly, for every realization of the signal s_2, the buyer of the asset is willing to pay in excess of her estimate of the value of future dividends, an amount that represents the option to resell in period 3 and that equals

$$b_2 = .25\delta^2 q(\theta_h - \theta_l). \tag{6}$$

This difference can be naturally called a (period 2) bubble and is a result of fluctuating differences of opinion and future opportunities to trade.

In order to model a bubble resulting from differences in beliefs and restrictions to short selling, it suffices to consider three periods. However, to examine bubble implosions as in section A.2, we need two periods in which an asset pricing bubble can potentially occur. For this reason, I consider four periods, but as I hope it becomes transparent, the reasoning in period $t = 1$ duplicates exactly the argument we used for period 2 above.

In fact, buyers at $t = 1$ are willing to bid for the asset an amount that reflects the sum of the dividends they expect the asset to pay and the value of the option of reselling the asset in future periods. For instance, the valuation of future dividends at $t = 1$ for a rational buyer is given by expression (1). However, the rational buyer is willing to pay at $t = 1$

$$\delta(\overline{\theta} + Ep_2). \tag{7}$$

The difference between (7) and (1) is

$$b_1 = .25(\delta^2 + \delta^3)q(\theta_h - \theta_l). \tag{8}$$

It is easy to check that (8) also expresses the difference between the reservation value of a B agent and her valuation of future dividends for every value of the signal s_1. Thus for every realization of the signal s_1, b_1 represents the amount that the buyer of the asset is willing to pay in excess of her estimate of the value of future dividends.

Since there is no bubble in period 3, we may set $b_3 = 0$ and a comparison of (6) and (8) establishes that:

$$b_1 > b_2 > b_3.$$

Bubbles decline over time because there are fewer opportunities to resell.

In this very simple model, we may think of the parameter q as a measure of differences in beliefs. After all, in periods $t = 1, 2, 3$, with probability $2q$ there are differences in beliefs once the signals s_t are observed. In addition, as argued above, agents in group B exaggerate the precision of their beliefs whenever $s_t \neq 1$. The event $s_t \neq 1$ has probability $2q$. Thus an increase in q also corresponds to an increase in the probability that agents in group B exhibit over-confidence. The size of the bubble in periods 1 or 2 is increasing as a function of q. Further, if we write

$$r = \frac{1}{\delta} - 1$$

for the (risk-free) interest rate implicit in the risk-free technology, then in periods 1 and 2 the bubble decreases with the risk-free interest rate.

The model discussed here has predictions on the effect of the difference in beliefs q on the volume of trade. For symmetry, suppose both groups are of the same size and at time 0 each group owns half of the supply of the risky asset. In period 1, with probability $2q$, all assets are bought by agents in one of the two groups, and with probability $1-2q$, $s_1 = 1$ and all agents agree on the distribution of dividends in the future, and thus there is no reason to trade. Hence, since S is the total supply of the asset, the average volume of trade in period 1 is

$$EV_1 = \frac{1}{2} \times 2q \times S = qS. \qquad (9)$$

If $s_1 = 2$ and $s_2 = 0$ or if $s_1 = 0$ and $s_2 = 2$, the group holding the risky asset in period 1 would sell it in period 2. The probability that $s_1 = 2$ and $s_2 = 0$ equals q^2, which is also the probability that $s_1 = 0$ and $s_2 = 2$. Also, trade will occur if $s_1 = 1$, and $s_2 = 0$ or $s_2 = 2$, but in this case, only half the assets would change hands. The probability of this event is $(1-2q)2q$. In all other cases no trade would occur in period 2. Thus the expected volume of trade in period 2 is

$$EV_2 = 2q^2 S + (1-2q)2q \times \frac{1}{2} \times S = qS. \qquad (10)$$

All shares will change hands in period 3, if $s_3 = 2$ and $s_2 = 0$ or if $s_3 = 0$ and $s_2 = 2$. In addition, all shares will change hands at $t = 3$ if the history of signals is $(0, 1, 2)$ or $(2, 1, 0)$. These four events have an aggregate probability $2q^2 + 2q^2(1-2q)$. In addition, trade will occur if the histories of the signals is

(1, 1, 2) or (1, 1, 0), and each of these events has probability $q(1-2q)^2$, but if histories (1, 1, 2) or (1, 1, 0) obtain, only half the shares will exchange hands at $t = 3$. Thus the average volume in period 3 is given by

$$EV_3 = 2q^2 S + 2q^2(1-2q)S + q(1-2q)^2 S = qS. \quad (11)$$

An examination of expressions (9) through (11) makes it evident that an increase in the parameter q increases the expected volume of trade in every period, just as it increases the value of the bubble. An increase in q raises the probability that the option to resell will be exercised (volume) and raises the value of that resale option (size of bubble).

I summarize these results in a Proposition:

Proposition 1. In the presence of fluctuating differences in beliefs and short-sale constraints, bubbles exist; investors are willing to pay for an asset in excess of their own valuation of future dividends. In addition,

  i. The size of the bubble increases when the probability of disagreement increases.
 ii. The volume of trade also increases with the probability of disagreement.
iii. The size of the bubble decreases with the risk-free interest rate.
 iv. The bubble declines as the time of maturity of the asset approaches, because there are fewer opportunities to trade.

A.2 LIMITED CAPITAL

It is straightforward to incorporate more periods into the model or treat a stationary model with infinite horizon. The introduction of risk-aversion complicates substantially the computations. However as Hong et al. (2006) showed, in a model of heterogeneous beliefs and costly short sale with risk-averse agents, the bubble and asset turnover rate decrease as the supply of the asset increases and bubbles may implode when float unexpectedly increases. The intuition is that as their holdings of the asset increase, risk-averse agents have a smaller marginal valuation for the asset and, as a consequence, it takes a bigger difference in opinions for the whole asset supply to change hands. An alternative that displays the same relationships between float, bubbles, and turnover as when agents are risk averse, albeit in a less continuous manner, is to adopt the short-cut proposed by Allen and Gale (2002) of limited capital and cash-in-the-market-pricing. Each group of agents will have the same preferences and views on signals as in appendix A.1, but here I no longer assume that the wealth of agents in both groups is so large that they can always acquire the full supply of the risky asset at their own valuation. The demand for the risky asset by a group of agents will be limited by the liquidity in their hands.

Before trading in period t, but after receiving period t dividends, agents in group $C \in \{A, B\}$ will have an aggregate portfolio (S_{t-1}^C, K_t^C). Here S_{t-1}^C is the amount of the risky asset they chose to hold in period $t-1$ and $K_t^C > 0$ is the cash available to them. K_t^C is a result of investments in the risk-free technology in period $t-1$, period t dividends on risky-asset holdings, and any (net) risk-free borrowing the agents in group C may access. Below, I will deduce each group's portfolio holdings before trading in period t, as a function of their initial holdings (S_0^C, K_0^C), portfolio decisions, and the realizations of signals and dividends; but at this point I treat these portfolios as exogenous.

Write v_t^C for the (marginal) valuation that agents in group $C \in \{A, B\}$ have for the risky asset at time t. More specifically, v_t^C equals the maximum price-per-unit that an agent in group C that has a positive income is willing to pay for an infinitesimal amount of the asset. This amount is a function of the expectations that the agent has concerning dividends and prices in period $t+1$. The limitation imposed by liquidity constraints on demand may yield lower equilibrium prices than those derived in appendix A.1 and thus cause the marginal valuation of some agents to be smaller than the marginal valuations deduced in appendix A.1.

Write S_t for the total supply of the asset at t. To simplify matters, I will assume that there is enough capital in the hands of group A agents so that at time t they can acquire the whole supply not yet in the hands of group A agents, $S_t - S_{t-1}^A$, at their valuation v_t^A. That is, I assume that

$$\frac{K_t^A}{S_t - S_{t-1}^A} > v_t^A. \tag{12}$$

Notice that inequality (12) involves the portfolios held by group A agents and the valuation of A agents, v_t^A. However one may replace v_t^A in the r.h.s. of (12) by the (larger) valuation of the risky asset by A agents that was already calculated in appendix A.1, and the denominator $S_t - S_{t-1}^A$ by S_t. This stronger assumption would imply inequality (12).

I will assume, however, that agents in group B have more limited capital. Suppose in period t, group B agents have a valuation v_t^B for the risky asset, while the valuation of A agents is v_t^A. If $v_t^A \geq v_t^B$, then the price of the asset $p_t = v_t^A$ since inequality (12) insures that group A agents have sufficient capital to acquire the total supply S_t at their valuation v_t^A. If $\frac{K_t^B}{(S_t - S_{t-1}^B)} \geq v_t^B > v_t^A$, then B agents would bid up the price, until $p_t = v_t^B$, since in this case group B agents have sufficient capital to acquire the risky assets not in their hands at their own valuation. If $v_t^A \leq \frac{K_t^B}{(S_t - S_{t-1}^B)} < v_t^B$, then the marginal buyer would belong to group B, but because of the liquidity constraints on group B agents, the price is

$$p_t = \frac{K_t^B}{(S_t - S_{t-1}^B)}.$$

In the language of Allen and Gale (2002), cash-in-the-market-pricing obtains; the price of the asset is determined by the liquidity available to group B agents. Finally, if $v_t^A > \frac{K_t^B}{(S_t - S_{t-1}^B)}$ then the marginal buyer is necessarily in group A and $p_t = v_t^A$. Thus:

$$p_t = \max\left\{ v_t^A, \min\left\{ v_t^B, \frac{K_t^B}{S_t - S_{t-1}^B} \right\} \right\}.$$

Other things equal, this price decreases as S_t increases. For instance, the larger is the float in period 1, S_1, relative to the initial holding of the B group, the lower would be the initial price p_1. If the float in period 1 is large enough, then even when B agents are optimists some of the asset's supply ends up in the hands of A agents, because of the limited capital of group B agents. In fact, when B agents are optimists, but the marginal buyer is an A agent, the amount that ends in the hands of B agents, S_1^B, solves:

$$v_1^A = \frac{K_1^B}{\left(S_1^B - S_0^B\right)}.$$

In this way, a larger float lowers the price and the turnover of the asset. If the supply of the risky asset remains constant through time, an asset with a larger float will also have a smaller turnover in subsequent periods.

To study the effect of an increase in the supply of the risky asset in period 2, we will first consider the price that would prevail in period 3. When $s_3 = 2$ (group B agents are optimists) $v_3^B > v_3^A$. If $K_3^B \geq (S_3 - S_2^B)v_3^B$, then group B agents will bid up the price of the asset to their valuation v_3^B and acquire the full supply. However, if $s_3 = 2$ but $K_3^B < (S_3 - S_2^B)v_3^B$, group B agents do not have enough wealth to buy the full supply of the risky asset at their valuation v_3^B. In this case, if they buy the full supply, the maximum group B agents can pay for a unit of the asset is $\frac{K_3^B}{S_3 - S_2^B}$. If the price group B agents can afford when they acquire the full supply in the hands of group A exceeds the valuation of group A agents, that is, $\frac{K_3^B}{S_3 - S_2^B} > v_3^A = \delta\bar{\theta}$, then the equilibrium price when $s_3 = 2$ is $\frac{K_3^B}{S_3 - S_2^B}$. Finally if $\frac{K_3^B}{S_3 - S_2^B} < \delta\bar{\theta} = v_3^A$, some of the asset is held by group

A agents, even though $s_3 = 2$, and thus the price of the risky asset must equal $\delta\bar{\theta}$. The price p_3 when $s_3 = 2$ is a (weakly) decreasing function of S_3 and equals $\delta\bar{\theta}$ if the supply of the asset in period 3 is large enough. Since $p_3 = \delta\bar{\theta}$ whenever $s_3 \neq 2$, the average price in period 3, Ep_3, is also a (weakly) decreasing function of S_3 and equals $\delta\bar{\theta}$, if the supply of the asset in period 3 is large enough, when compared to the holdings of B agents in period 2. This contrasts with the case without limited capital, when Ep_3 would always exceed $\delta\bar{\theta}$ (c.f. equation (2) above).

Buyers of the stock of the South Sea Company or buyers of Internet stocks in the late 1990s did not know with certainty the future supply of these assets. One can model this uncertainty in a simple way by assuming that supply may increase in period 2. Suppose $S_0 = S_1 = S$, and that $S_3 = S_2 = S$ with probability π and equals $S + \Delta S > S$ with probability $1 - \pi$. Suppose further that the realization of the supply of the risky asset is independent of all dividends and signals and that the supply realization is observed in period 2 before the signal s_2 is observed. Since trading in period 2 occurs after s_2 is observed, investors know the actual supply when they trade in period 2. While the amount S is held from the beginning by agents in groups A and B, any increase in supply will come from sales of the asset by "insiders," as in Hong et al. (2006). To simplify matters, I will assume that insiders only wish to sell.[3]

I will show that for certain parameter values, a bubble exists before period 2. In addition, the bubble persists in periods 2 and 3 if the supply does not increase, but deflates in period 2 if the supply increases. The deflation of the bubble in period 2 will be a consequence of the realization by all investors that, because of the supply increase and the limited aggregate wealth of group B agents, the marginal buyer in period 3 will necessarily be rational even when $s_3 = 2$, and the irrational agents are optimists. The occurrence of this scenario will depend on the wealth of group B agents in period 3 and the supply they would have to absorb in that same period to guarantee that the price exceeds the valuation of the rational buyers. I will start by imposing some bounds on the aggregate portfolio of group B agents that will insure that the bubble persists when the supply of the asset is unchanged and the bubble deflates when the supply increases, and will later show that these bounds would hold when the initial supply of the risky asset, S, is sufficiently small and the potential increase in the supply in period 2, ΔS, is sufficiently large.

Suppose that the capital constraints of group B only bind in period 3 when the supply increases:

$$\frac{K_3^B}{S - S_2^B} \geq \delta[\bar{\theta} + .25(\theta_h - \theta_l)], \qquad (13)$$

and that when the capital constraints bind, they are strong enough, that is:

$$\frac{K_3^B}{S + \Delta S - S_2^B} < \delta\bar{\theta}. \qquad (14)$$

Equation (13) guarantees that if supply does not increase in period 2, $S_2 = S$ and the signal observed in period 3 $s_3 = 2$, the demand by group B agents will drive the price of the asset in period 3 to v_3^B and thus exceed the expected "rational" payoff in period 3. Inequality (14) insures that if S_2 increases to $S + \Delta S$, the price of the asset in period 3 will equal the (discounted) average payoff expected by rational agents, since a member of group A would necessarily be the marginal buyer of the asset.[4]

Thus when $S_2 = S$, the price in period 3 matches exactly the price when there are no capital constraints, whereas when $S_2 = S + \Delta S$ the price in period 3 equals the valuation of the rational agents, independent of the signal. In particular, if the supply of the asset increases in period 2 because of sales by insiders, that is $S_2 = S + \Delta S$, there is no period 2 bubble, since it is known that period 3 prices are independent of the signal s_3 that is observed. On the other hand, if supply of the asset does not increase in period 2, then, as in the case of no capital constraints,

$$Ep_3 = \delta[\overline{\theta} + .25q(\theta_h - \theta_l)],$$

reflecting the fact that B agents would acquire the whole float if $s_3 = 2$.

In order to guarantee that if $S_2 = S$ prices in period 2 would be exactly as in the case of no capital constraints, we need to insure that

$$\frac{K_2^B}{S - S_1^B} \geq (\delta + \delta^2)[\overline{\theta} + .25q(\theta_h - \theta_l)]. \tag{15}$$

Inequality (15) guarantees that when $s_2 = 2$ and $S_2 = S$, B agents will acquire the full float of the asset.

To insure that when $S_2 = S + \Delta S$ the marginal buyer of the asset always belongs to group A, it suffices that:

$$\frac{K_2^B}{S + \Delta S - S_1^B} \leq (\delta + \delta^2)\overline{\theta}. \tag{16}$$

If inequalities (13) and (16) hold, then before S_2 (and hence s_2) is observed

$$Ep_2 = (\delta + \delta^2)[\overline{\theta} + .25q\pi(\theta_b - \theta_l)],$$

reflecting the fact that a bubble would occur in period 2 if and only if the supply stays constant. In addition when inequalities (13) and (15) hold, rational buyers in period 1 will always be willing to pay in excess of their own valuations of future dividends of the risky asset, because if supply does not increase they may have an opportunity to sell the asset to over-optimistic B agents. Since we have assumed that group A agents have sufficient capital to buy the total supply of the asset at these higher prices, the price of the asset in period 1 exceeds the expected discounted dividends independently of the realized signal in period 1 (s_1) and the capital constraints of group B agents.

When $s_1 = 2$, group B valuation at time 1 is

$$v_1^B(2) = \delta(\overline{\theta} + .25q(\theta_b - \theta_l) + (\delta + \delta^2)[\overline{\theta} + .25q\pi(\theta_b - \theta_l)]),$$

which again exceeds the present value of dividends expected by group B agents by $(\delta + \delta^2)[\overline{\theta} + .25q\pi(\theta_b - \theta_l)]$. To guarantee that the price in period 1 when $s_1 = 2$ is observed equals $v_1^B(2)$, one must assume that:

$$\frac{K_1^B}{S - S_0^B} \geq v_1^B(2). \tag{17}$$

In this case, there will be a bubble in period 1, independently of the signal s_1 observed and $b_1 = .25(\delta + \delta^2)q\pi(\theta_h - \theta_l)$, which is smaller than the bubble that obtains when liquidity constraints are not binding—equation (8)—reflecting the possibility that future supplies may increase. However, as $\pi \to 1$, the probability that future supplies increase goes to zero and the value of the bubbles under the two liquidity scenarios converge to each other.

Until now I took the portfolio held by group B agents after the payment of dividends in periods 1 to 3 as given and assumed that inequalities (14) through (17) hold. Agents in group B start with a non-negative initial endowment of $S_0^B < S$ units of the risky asset and K_0^B units of the good, and the values $S_{t-1}^B \leq S$ and K_t^B for t = 2, 3 are consequences of their actions, realizations of the random shocks and equilibrium prices in period 1 and 2. Furthermore, for a given K_0^B it is straightforward to show that inequalities (13), (15), and (17) hold, whenever S is small enough. The intuition underlying this result is that if S is small enough, even if B agents acquire the full supply of the risky asset and have no possibility of borrowing, they would have a minimum amount left over to invest in the risk-free technology. This delivers a lower bound on K_1^B, K_2^B, and K_3^B, the amounts available to agents in group B to acquire additional shares in periods 1 to 3. By assuming an even smaller value for S, if necessary, we can thus guarantee that inequalities (13), (15), and (17) hold.

I now show that inequalities (14) and (16) always hold provided ΔS is large enough and agents in group B have no access to borrowing in addition to the amount that is already reflected in their initial liquidity K_0^B. To accomplish this, we have to study the dynamics of the evolution of the aggregate wealth of B agents. Given K_0^B and S_0^B, the evolution of the aggregate wealth of group B in equilibrium depends on the realizations of the dividends, signals and supply, and on the way assets are allocated between the two groups when their valuations are identical. I assume that when the two groups have identical valuations for the risky asset, group B agents get all the shares they want.[5] Write $W_t^B(K_0^B, S_0^B)$ for the maximum wealth that agents in group B can have after dividend payments in period t, where the maximum is taken over all possible realizations of signals, dividends, and all portfolio choices. Notice that an increase in ΔS cannot increase W_1^B or W_2^B, because the price of the risky asset can only decrease with an increase in ΔS. The price of the asset in period 2 is not less than $(\delta + \delta^2)\bar{\theta}$, the expected (by A agents) discounted dividends of the asset. If ΔS is large enough,

$$W_2^B < (\delta + \delta^2)\bar{\theta}\frac{S + \Delta S}{2} \le p_2 \frac{S + \Delta S}{2}.$$

Even if B agents use all their wealth in period 2 to buy the asset they cannot acquire more than half the total (larger) supply, and thus (16) holds and,

$$S_2^B < \frac{S + \Delta S}{2}. \tag{18}$$

Thus, if the supply increases, the marginal buyer in period 2 is necessarily an A agent. Further, the *ex-post* rate of return of the risky asset between periods 2 and 3 will depend on the price of the asset that prevails in periods 2 and 3 and the realization of the dividend θ_3. Since the price of the risky asset in period 3 is at most the expected (by B agents) discounted dividends of the asset when $s_3 = 2$, and the dividend paid is at most θ_h, the rate of return is at most

$$\overline{R} := \frac{\theta_h + \delta(\overline{\theta} + .25(\theta_h - \theta_l))}{(\delta + \delta^2)\overline{\theta}}$$

Notice that this bound exceeds $1 + r$ and thus is also a bound for the growth in wealth. Hence,

$$W_3^B \le \overline{R} W_2^B$$

and, since W_2^B can only decrease with ΔS, by choosing if necessary a larger ΔS we can insure that

$$K_3^B \le W_3^B \le \overline{R} W_2^B \le \delta\overline{\theta}\frac{\Delta S}{2} < \delta\overline{\theta}(S + \Delta S - S_2^B),$$

where the last inequality follows from equation (18). Hence inequality (14) holds, and, in particular, the price of the asset in period 3 equals the average payoff expected by A agents.

Thus in the model in this section, a bubble arises in period 1 provided that "irrational" agents have enough initial wealth relative to the initial supply of the risky asset, and the bubble implodes in period 2 if and only if the supply of the risky asset increases by a sufficiently large amount in period 2.

COMMENTARY

PATRICK BOLTON

Let me begin by saying that it is a great honor for me to be commenting on José Scheinkman's paper. José is a friend and a co-author. I have the absolute highest respect and admiration for his research and the work that he presents here. It was also a truly special honor sharing this opportunity to write on stock market bubbles and financial crises with three giants of economic theory.

José's exploration of the economic foundations of stock market bubbles is quite a tour de force. He has already referred to contributions by Ken, Joe, and Sanford, and I will be doing just the same. In my comments I am going to attempt to put the ideas that José discussed into context. Specifically, I am going to emphasize the importance of the work of four economists and four economic theories. I also want to underline—more than José did—the backdrop of the efficient-markets hypothesis, which remains the dominant paradigm in finance. For the purposes of my comments, my definition of the efficient-markets hypothesis (which I am phrasing somewhat differently from the usual definition)

is that equilibrium asset prices generally reflect the long-
term fundamental value of assets; they neither deviate much
below this value, nor above, so that only very limited arbi-
trage gains can be reaped at any time.

One major crack in that efficient-markets edifice has been
opened up by the classic contribution of Sanford Grossman
and Joseph Stiglitz (1980), who pointed out that if the fundamental value of assets is unknown, and any research to
determine the value of future cash flows is costly to produce,
then equilibrium prices cannot fully reflect all the available
information. In fact, all kinds of things can go wrong once
you make that observation. No trade outcomes can emerge
once trading parties are known to trade under asymmetric
information. How do you get informed people to trade with
uninformed people? You can only get trade in the presence
of noise traders, agents who wish to trade no matter what the
price is at which they trade.

The noise trader is just a convenient modeling device, but
one fruitful way of thinking about noise traders in reality is
as traders with different opinions. This is the direction José
has taken in his classic 2003 article with Wei Xiong in the
Journal of Political Economy. In that article he and Wei build
on insights first articulated by John Maynard Keynes and
later formalized by Harrison and Kreps (1978), and propose
the formal foundations for what I would argue is an alternative, broader view of financial markets; what I am tempted to
refer to as the speculative-markets hypothesis in opposition
to efficient-markets hypothesis.

As José explains in his lecture, there are two essential ingre-
dients that go into this framework: 1) a simple behavioral

bias for investors, a form of over-confidence, which induces investors to attach too much informational content to some signals they receive about the value of an asset. This over-confidence is the source of differences of opinion among investors, as different investors are over-confident about different signals; 2) speculation (or betting between investors with different opinions), which naturally arises from investors' differences of opinion. This speculation is the source of asset price bubbles—when it is easier to take a long position in an asset than a short position—for then the demand by optimists tends to outweigh the supply by pessimists, thus giving rise to inflated asset prices. What is more, when asset prices vary over time with the beliefs of the most optimistic investors, demand for assets can be purely speculative and may no longer be anchored to the fundamental value of the asset; buyers may choose to hold an asset purely on the expectation that a quick profit can be obtained by selling the asset to a more optimistic buyer in the future. In other words, as Scheinkman and Xiong (2003) establish in their model that underpins the speculative-markets hypothesis, the price of a stock at any moment in time is the sum of the fundamental value of the asset plus a speculative option value. This speculative option value is really what we can think of as a bubble.

While mainstream finance scholarship of the past fifty years has embraced the efficient-markets hypothesis, this is much less the case for economic historians, who have studied financial crises in the past. Some notion of a speculative-markets hypothesis is typically adopted by most economic historians. However, historians' explanations of bubbles and

Used with permission of Kevin KAL Kallaugher, Kaltoons.com.

crises have been thought to be too vague to be combinable with quantitative models of financial markets. This is one important reason why historical accounts have had little traction in modern finance theory. Consider the cartoon above. The caption reads "just a normal day at the nation's most important financial institution."

Why am I referring to it? Because, as revealing as the cartoon is of a reality in financial markets, to a finance scholar this is not a particularly helpful cartoon. What do you do with this insight? How do you go on from here? Often, when we read economic history discussions of bubbles, of manias and panics, we understand the idea of manias and panics, but what's the next step? The rigorous, mathematically-founded model of Scheinkman and Xiong (2003) may, admittedly, not exactly represent what historians had in mind when they talk about manias and panics. But in my view, the merit of the model is precisely to define notions like bubbles accurately and thus to facilitate their integration in quantitative models of financial markets.

Let me further contrast the theory of Scheinkman and Xiong with the explanations of financial crises put forward by the economic historians Charles P. Kindleberger and Robert Aliber in their leading text, *Manias, Panics, and Crashes: A History of Financial Crises* (1978). Throughout his career, Charles Kindleberger went after the following big questions: What causes crises? Is there a pattern, and if you can identify the pattern, can crises be prevented? How do we deal with such crises? Kindleberger and Aliber portray past episodes of financial crises mostly in terms of manias followed by panics, not unlike the irrational behavior of investors described in the cartoon. But it also offers other more rational explanations. In particular, it emphasizes the role of lax monetary policy and financial deregulation in facilitating the emergence of manias.

While the Scheinkman and Xiong theory can explain how manias emerge (and how crashes may follow bubbles), the model is too simple to be able to explain the persistence and amplification of bubbles; why bubble episodes may last several years, as opposed to a few days or weeks. Kindleberger and Aliber offer a number of explanations for the persistence of bubbles, which nicely complement the Scheinkman and

Xiong theory. A first factor they mention is how during manias optimistic beliefs are often backed by 'new economy' illusions: investors base their optimistic projections on the belief that new general-purpose technologies (new sources of energy, modes of transport, the advent of personal computers, the Internet, etc.) will transform the economy and provide permanent new sources of profits. Another effect that often fuels manias is the idea that investors are induced to rush into new investments on the reasoning that they'd better "get on the train before it leaves the station." Related to this effect, they also mention repeatedly that during manias investors justify their purchases of new assets simply on the anticipation of short-term capital gains, which is basically the same as Scheinkman and Xiong's speculative option value. Another interesting explanation they put forward is a form of chicken-and-egg mechanism: more investments become profitable when the cost of capital goes down, and the cost of capital in turn goes down (valuations go up) as investors forecast higher earnings-growth options. This mechanism can also generate bubble-and-crashe cycles quite easily. Then, they explain how herd behavior has often been a source of amplification of manias and crashes, with uninformed or ignorant investors stepping in and out of particular asset classes, simply on the basis of the behavior of other investors, who are perceived to be better informed. And finally they stress the importance of leverage, and lending booms, in amplifying and prolonging manias and crashes. In particular, they explain how fund managers tend to resort to leverage as a way of boosting returns for their investors as the bubble peaks.

Turning points of bubbles are very hard to predict. That is the inevitable nature of financial markets, whether investors have differences of opinions or not. For if future turning points were predictable, they would simply be brought forward in time by investors and cease to be predictable. This is, alas, not a very encouraging observation for future financial regulators, and those charged with identifying and predicting systemic risk.

However, as José has pointed out, there may be some early warning signs of an ongoing bubble and an impending crash, but one has to go beyond the observation of prices and look at changes in supply of a particular asset. If there are significant and sustained upward deviations from trend in the supply of a particular asset—as we have witnessed during the technology bubble with new offers of technology stocks, or during the subprime crisis with new offers of subprime mortgage-backed securities—this may well be evidence of an ongoing bubble. Another red flag is that the math in some valuations, or growth projections, just doesn't add up. For example, in the Japan stock bubble at the end of the 1980s, the stock market capitalization of Japanese companies was twice the stock market capitalization of U.S. companies, but Japanese GDP was then less than half of U.S. GDP. It was all based on dubious growth projections.

While much of the focus of Kindleberger and Aliber's book is on manias, they also make important observations on crashes and how crashes also tend to overshoot. The Scheinkman and Xiong model is again too stylized to allow for overshooting in crashes, but I suspect that it could be augmented to allow for such overshooting. A

central phenomenon in this respect stressed by Kindleberger and Aliber is flight to quality. When investors
realize that they have been too optimistic they lose faith
in their ability to make accurate valuations and seek out
safe places to protect their wealth, such as cash, treasuries
or, possibly, gold (when even treasuries are seen as risky).
Here is how I interpret flight to quality: following a crash,
it is as if investors needed to 'reboot' their belief formation
process, forget about their wrong 'new economy' assumptions, and redefine their prior beliefs, before they are again
ready to return to stock markets and process new information based on a newly formed paradigm (or prior beliefs).
There is a whole new angle in the formation of investors'
beliefs here to explore—and what the implications are for
asset prices.

To conclude, I would just like to raise three general questions for the theory, which I think are going to be critical in
pushing the theory forward and more into the mainstream.
The first question is something that José alluded to in his
lecture: how do we make welfare judgements when investors
have different opinions driven by over-confidence? Do we
need to return to some form of paternalism? If we are aware
that people may be over-confident and that they may get car-
ried away and come to regret it, should we step in and stop
them from doing what they might regret afterwards? That is
a difficult question. I am not sure that we necessarily want to
go down that path or if we do, how far we want to go. But it
is an important question when it comes to financial regulation. For example, John Paulson, the hedge-fund manager,

made a fortune by shorting subprime mortgage-backed securities. One might argue, as many commentators have, that this was a welcome development because through his trades he imposed discipline in the housing market and thereby lessened misallocation of resources to that market. On the other hand, who was transacting with Paulson? German banks and other investors who believed it was fine to buy assets from him (whether directly or indirectly through an intermediary). Most likely they were not fully aware of what he was doing and how he was structuring deals like Abacus. So one might have some doubts there. That is the welfare question. I do not know how to resolve it, but it seems to me to be a major question to address.

My second question is, how do we think about asset management for pension funds and other long-term investors in the presence of bubbles and short-term speculative markets? That is a completely wide-open agenda. We need to revisit the notion that maximizing short-term returns is equivalent to maximizing long-term returns in light of the Scheinkman and Xiong speculative-markets hypothesis.

A third question that is perhaps a little bit more technical concerns credit bubbles. As José has pointed out, it is very difficult to have bubbles with finite maturity fixed-income securities. As the evidence on the Chinese warrants bubble by Wei Xiong and Jialin Yu (2011) reveals, bubbles tend to disappear as the security approaches maturity. How, then, do credit bubbles emerge, if debt has finite maturity? I wonder whether the credit bubbles we have seen may in fact be tied to an underlying asset bubble for the collateral, as we have seen with housing and mortgages. In the case of mortgages, although the borrower has to repay at a certain date, he can always refinance based on the value of the house. Thus the only thing that matters in this case is the projected value of the house.

COMMENTARY

I first met José Scheinkman when I was a teenager in graduate school. I met Joseph Stiglitz soon after and then Kenneth Arrow. They were all very important influences in my
life, so it gives me great pleasure to be around them again.

The topic of this book reminds me of the Supreme Court
justice, Potter Stewart, who said something along the lines
of: I cannot really define what I understand to be pornography, but I know it when I see it. Bubbles to me are a little bit like that. Again, sometimes you see a movie and the
issue is not whether it is pornography, but whether you have
enjoyed it. In the case of José's paper, the issue is not whether
it was about bubbles, but whether we have gotten insights
and pleasure out of it, which I certainly have.

I will start by discussing the definitions of bubbles that he
listed, beginning with the point that asset prices exceed an
asset's fundamental value. Well, if only you could figure out
what an asset's fundamental value is! That is actually quite a
bit of work. As Patrick Bolton alluded to, Joe and I wrote a
paper in 1980 exploring that, given that it is very hard work

to figure out the fundamental value of an asset, it is unlikely that all assets are going to be priced at their fundamental value, because no one will get a return from doing so. It cannot be very easy even from a scientific point of view ex-post, not to mention ex-ante, of determining whether assets were at their fundamental value. I think this is a fundamentally empirically useless kind of definition, because you simply cannot tell whether an asset is at its fundamental value, anymore than you can objectively define pornography.

The next definition we have of a bubble is that asset prices exceed fundamentals because owners believe they can resell the asset for a higher price in the future. Yet most people who buy assets actually do so for the purposes of selling it for a higher price in the future. In general, you would expect price appreciation in a world in which earnings grow. The price is going to rise (and you expect that) if there is no current dividend; your return has to have a capital gain component. It is surely not the definition of speculation that people buy something because they think they are going to sell it at a higher price.

Then José presents what I think is quite a unique and innovative definition: If you do not have short sales, then anyone who is long is, in effect, acquiring a resale option and that has value. Maybe asset prices are higher than they otherwise would have been on average because of the resale option inherent in being long. One might try to follow this up and say that if we simply had a law against short sales, then we would all be wealthier because asset prices would all be higher. But if you think about that, you would see that something is not quite right.

Jose's quote from Tom Wolfe was really insightful and appropriate because Wolfe's book is actually about the art market. Imagine you look at a Jeff Koons or an Andy Warhol picture of a Campbell's soup can and you say, well, can that really be selling for more than a Rembrandt? I might ask that question, but other people might say, well, that Rembrandt is old-style art and this is new-style art, and such differences in opinion are typical of asset valuations as well as art valuations. Wolfe describes all of the critics in the art market, and they are very similar to José's description of the analysts and consultants in the asset market. You could take the mathematics of the paper literally and write it as a model of the modern art market.

But bubbles are not really about the art market. Who really cared that Jeff Koons went down 25% in auction value in 2008 versus 2007? I do not think that really bothered people very much. The fact that some particular thing that was overpriced became less overpriced is not exactly what financial crises or bubbles are about.

The real issue is excessive risk-taking. What we ex-post consider a bubble was in fact a situation in which there was really excessive risk-taking that went wrong. Generally, risk-taking eventually goes wrong, but when excessive risk-taking goes wrong, it goes wrong excessively. If the risk-taking is truly excessive, as we had in the period leading up to 2008, then when it goes wrong, it goes severely wrong. This is not dissimilar to a lot of the points that Patrick made, and I will cover leverage below.

The savings and loan crisis of the early 1990s has been almost forgotten, because it was a minor crisis when compared to the crisis we had in 2008. At the time many people thought it was really bad. People thought it would lead to a quite severe recession, which it did. It was severe and sharp, but it ended very quickly. This was a situation where we had excessive risk-taking associated with excessive leverage. The leverage came because the savings- and loan-banks could borrow at the risk-free rate because of FDIC insurance and then proceeded to make very risky investments.

I will return to the issue of taking advantage of optionality and compensation, which is something similar to what José described as a source of excessive risk-taking and as another element that can cause a bad event, which we might or might not want to call a bubble. By definition, there were definitely prices that were too high in the savings and loan crisis, but the reason that we remember it as a crisis, and that it had negative effects on GDP growth, was the excessive leverage.

There are situations where you can separate out the issue of excessive leverage, and excessive risk-taking, from the issue of huge classes of assets that are over-valued. The huge classes of assets that are over-valued are the symptom, not the cause. In the savings and loan crisis, you saw the actual cause, which was the excessive leverage, leading to bankruptcy and leading to a reduction in credit and ultimately a recession.

If we think a bubble is excessive leverage and risk-taking, which we look back on ex-post after they have gone wrong, then we must ask how we get the excessive leverage. To have a really big fire, it is most important to have a lot of fuel. Similarly, leverage is really crucial to these issues. As we have become financially more sophisticated, we have found more and more sophisticated ways to create and generate leverage.

When we look back on the financial crisis or the dotcom bubble, we see them as important because of the systemic nature of the leverage involved and the systemic nature of the consequences of the bad states that occurred in the excessive risk-taking. If you go back to 1999, there was no scientific proof that all of these companies would not have succeeded. Companies were being valued on clicks—how many people actually went to the website—not earnings, so you would have the price of a company based on web traffic. Analysts would report price-to-click ratios. Maybe that seemed right at the time; it turned out to be wrong. Most of what we look upon as a bubble is actually looking back ex-post at excessive risk-taking. I will discuss why there was excessive risk-taking there below and then find a certain stage where it went wrong.

Prior to the stock market crash in 1929, the industrial growth in America was amazing. In the period of 1880 through 1929, there was an amazing amount of risk-taking and a few crashes; ultimately one of them, the last one, was quite large The risk-taking was quite successful, and it changed a country from an agricultural country into the major industrial power in the world.

Looking at China today and at the value of Chinese stock prices now compared to where they were in 2000, you could say all of the industry that has been created is excessive risk-taking. You could also say the opposite. In five years, if it is down 50% from where it is today, you would call it excessive; but if it is not, you would say it was rational. It would behoove us all to come up with some accurate scientific measure of valuation.

But the issue is really leverage, not valuation. Looking at the housing bubble, suppose housing prices had only gone up 50% of what they actually went up, but people were twice as leveraged as they actually were. I think the consequence of the bust would have been virtually the same, if not worse.

The negative consequence of the housing bust was that people had to reduce their consumption more than proportionately to the reduction in the real value of their wealth because of a phantom component to their wealth. The phantom component of their wealth was created by the economy-wide borrowing that excessively bid up the value of houses. Had consumers not been able to engage in borrowing to bid up the value of their houses, I do not think there would have been as much of an effect anywhere of the housing bust. In particular, had there been no leverage, you would not have had the financial crisis we had. Had there only been leverage at the consumer level, we would still have had the financial crisis that we had.

One obvious sort of leverage that people focus on is excessive debt. It is interesting that when you look back at the dotcom bubble, it was not a debt-fueled bubble. It was actually an equity-fueled bubble; this is an interesting and different kind of notion that reminds me of Paul Samuelson's (1958) overlapping generations model of money. How did companies finance themselves? They financed themselves by issuing equity. This was an amazing period, where instead of going to a bank to borrow, as in 2003 when the Fed dropped the interest rate so low, you actually borrowed by issuing equity. Equity has a moneyness to it. Indeed, earnings were generally negative, but you also had people who were worth a billion dollars in a financial sense because of the value of their equity.

The moneyness created by equity was the fuel to the fire. Going back to Samuelson's article, you can ask why the paper that is issued actually has any value. It is because you give it to the next generation, which is willing to hold it and give it to the next generation, which is willing to hold it and so on. The interesting thing is, when I first read that paper years ago, I said to myself that sounds great, so why don't I issue a paper like that? What's the cost of issuance? If you read Samuelson's article, there is no cost of issuance. People just hold it and then give it to someone else.

That was really the first serious, purely intellectual article that I ever read that was internally consistent about bubbles. "Money" was a piece of paper that had value because someone else was willing to hold it, which is amazing if you think about it. In my opinion, the paper had nothing to do with monetary policy and money. It was about speculation. José talks about the importance of supply. If supply were endogenous in Samuelson's model—namely anyone could issue that paper—it would drive the value to zero, because if something with no issuance cost has a positive value, everyone would issue it and the world would be totally flooded with it.

Patrick had mentioned the Japanese bubble economy, which is really interesting, because they had both kinds of fuel. They had enormous amounts of debt, and equity was being used as money. The valuations of stocks were incredibly high, but companies delivered nothing to shareholders. The price-to-earnings ratio was similar to what we had in the dotcom era. Real estate value-to-rental ratios were similar to what we saw in the dotcom era of price-to-earnings ratio. Japan had a banking system that was essentially insured by the government, which provides enormous incentives for free options and risk-taking. The moneyness of equity was added to that, and what was created was the bubble to end all bubbles.

There is no reason to believe that leverage-fueled excessive risk-taking will not recur. Excessive risk-taking is still being generated from two sources. The first source arises when the government insures the debts of financial institutions and incentivizes (via the institutions managers' obvious compensation options) the institutions to take huge amounts of risks. The second source is the moneyness of equity. How much of equity value is its moneyness? Trying to answer that question is quite difficult. It's almost like explaining why a Warhol or a Koons has value. You might not want them in your house to look at, but they do have a high resale value.

I will conclude with one ex-ante prediction of bubbles, over-valuations, and financial crises. Where do you see the greatest amount of leverage in the world right now? It is here in America, in our fiscal policy and the accumulation of our fiscal policies over a 30-year period. Think about the fact that real conflagrations require a lot of fuel. If you want to look for a bubble in the world that is developing or exists (as a shorting opportunity), then the thing that I would look for is a lot of fuel. Where is there a huge amount of leverage? Where is there a huge amount of potential for stressing the system? Rather than, for example Europe, which everyone is currently focused on, it the ratio of the U.S. debt (including the present value of unfunded entitlements) to GDP, that presents the largest potential for a global crisis.

COMMENTARY

KENNETH J. ARROW

I have been concerned about one aspect of the efficiency of general equilibrium: the distribution of risks and the idea of rational individual behavior in that context. Rational theory is a limited theory, as Patrick Bolton has said. One of my questions is what that rational theory means. Does it in fact exist? For various reasons, I now think that the concept of Arrow-Debreu securities, though technically correct within its formulation, is misleading. In it, you seek to insure yourself against all contingencies, and the securities observed in the market form a complicated way of meeting this need. The value of each security depends on random events—you can think of storms; but a more important source of random variation in the long run comes from technological innovations. The trouble is that I really don't know the effects of these random events on me or my heirs, or on some other party who seems to be totally unconnected with me.

Consider, for example, the repercussions on someone in another industry on my selling efforts. The nature of a complex economy implies that there is no reason for me to know that connection; indeed, the ability to carry out a complex system of exchanges when each individual has only local knowledge is frequently cited as one of the virtues of the market system. The informational assumption implicit in the Arrow-Debreu interpretation of the securities markets is, tell me what exogenous events happen, and I will tell you the effects on the entire system. Every individual is a general equilibrium analyst.

This issue came up in the work of somebody who has been somewhat neglected—not incorrectly on the whole—Oskar Morgenstern. In the 1930s, Morgenstern was the director of a business cycle research center in Vienna. He considered the hypothesis of complete foresight; in the absence of random variations, everyone could predict the future economy, and in particular, prices. He pointed out a problem. What each agent does would depend on his or her expectations. But then the future would be dependent on the expectations of others, so the expectations would be simultaneously determined. This is the same paradigm as that raised by Keynes in his example of the beauty contest (when winning depends on agreeing with others). In the usual formulation of markets, the price mechanism serves to coordinate beliefs. But, in the absence of futures markets, there is no reason for expectations to be rational.

Morgenstern gave an example, one which was really not very appropriate, drawn from a Sherlock Holmes story. Moriarty and Holmes each pick a destination. If it is the same, Holmes dies; otherwise he survives. Morgenstern noted that if either guesses the other's action correctly, he acts so as to make the other's action non-optimal. (There is no equilibrium in pure strategies.) This was supposed to show that there really could not be correct expectations. It is not an appropriate example because, as the payoffs are not concave functions, we are not surprised at the failure of an equilibrium to exist in the absence of concavity.

Morgenstern retracted from this position in his work with von Neumann, *Theory of Games and Economic Behavior* (1944). There was an equilibrium in mixed strategies (mixed strategies automatically concavify the payoffs).

But the question is, how can you get to that fixed point? If Holmes is slightly in error about Moriarty's mixed strategy, his optimal strategy is to choose one destination with probability 1. Therefore, there seems to be no stable learning process which converges to the equilibrium.

This problem of getting to an equilibrium in beliefs is a central issue in José's very illuminating lecture. The basic components are the belief structures of the individuals in the economy and their consequent behavior. The beliefs are mostly but not entirely rationally formed. Like other scholars, he wants to distinguish a rational group of players from noise traders, an irrational group who exaggerate the values of signals.

The trouble is, as Morgenstern originally argued, that there is already an infinite regress. Once I form my beliefs, you form yours; my beliefs will alter to reflect the behavior induced by your beliefs, and so on. Game theorists have indeed shown that this process can be made consistent. That is what is behind such arguments as, "agreeing to disagree."

However, following Grossman and Stiglitz (1980), there is a process, and it may well be infinitely costly. Furthermore, the process depends on assuming that others are using the same inference process that you are. Analysts must recognize the cost of information. The failure to do so is the fundamental deficiency in all the ideas that you can have efficient markets involving the future without actually having futures markets. The simple notions derived from observing contemporary markets with no credit or uncertainty do not survive once you introduce the cost of information.

There is a further question: What is meant by individual rationality in the context of uncertainty? In the standard analysis of rational behavior under uncertainty, due to Leonard J. Savage (1954) (anticipated in part by Frank Ramsey), there is a fundamental arbitrariness, the choice of prior probabilities. These may, of course, differ among individuals.

One might say that there has been available a long time series of observations, so that, starting from almost any reasonable prior, the posteriors will converge to the same limit. First of all, that time may be very long indeed. More importantly, the economy is evolving; technological and financial innovation occurs so that the relevant observations are few. "You never step into the same river twice" (Heraclitus).

We have had commercial crises, in the modern sense, certainly since the first quarter of the 19th century. John Stuart Mill's *Principles of Political Economy* (1848) has a chapter on commercial crises, which is a pretty good description of what is happening now, allowing for institutional changes: credit is suddenly unavailable. The chapter does not offer much of an explanation; it is essentially a description and is not at all integrated with the rest of the book or with either his predecessor, David Ricardo, or his neoclassical successors.

The Long-Term Capital Management crisis, it seems to me, raises some questions about the working of credit "markets." (I use the quotes because the transactions are based on individual contracts, not on a market with generally known prices.) That LTCM engaged in risky transactions which resulted in failure may be perfectly rational. The expected value may have been high enough to compensate for the low perceived probability of failure. The real question is the rationality of the lenders, in particular, their acceptance of the high leverage. This is why I think Sanford's comments are so important. Leverage is what takes a disturbance and multiplies it. Who are the lenders? They are not ignorant people; they can't be put into the category of "noise traders." The effect is similar to the old-fashioned bank run, but the players are totally different. They are highly informed, they have a lot at stake, and they are professionals.

There are questions on my mind to which I do not know the answer. The lenders had a lot at stake, they lost big, and the consequences affected remote people. I personally invested in ordinary stocks. I would not dream of going into those mortgage-backed securities, particularly when every business newspaper was asking how long the housing boom could last. As a result, I lost 40% of my wealth, although I thought I was avoiding these risks. LTCM's failure was a systemic problem because the lenders had so much at stake.

In José's paper, the model is described by a series of equations, all of which look very smooth. The randomness is described by Brownian motion; with probability 1, any realization is a continuous function. These conditions would seem to imply that, if the economy starts to go down, there will be time for adjustments to take place. The model does not describe the bursting of a bubble. It is the suddenness of the burst that we need to explain. If the price of an asset represents in any sense its value, it is not credible that it decline by 50% in a few days, particularly if the asset is a physical investment or an equity. This is something other than rational anticipations. In fact, not only do prices go down abruptly but the market may disappear completely.

I have acquaintances who come from a physics background; for them, everything is a complex system. Somehow, it is characteristic of complex systems that probability distributions are thick-tailed, not normal. (I must confess that I still do not understand the reasons.) The probability of a catastrophic episode remains relatively high as we go to higher levels. In fact, in the last few years, the decreases in value have fallen even more drastically than would be expected from a Pareto distribution.

The real question is not, was there some leverage, but rather why leverage went to such extremes. Why did the lenders lend when they saw that 97 cents of every dollar invested by LTCM was their money (collectively)? One would expect them to ask LTCM to have more of its money at stake.

I think José correctly emphasizes that a belief system and a rational information system are not the same, even apart from the logical difficulties that I have raised. I once read a survey article in a psychological journal that if there is one thoroughly established psychological generalization, it is over-confidence in one's beliefs or other aspects of the self. When someone is asked to rank himself or herself in kindliness or intelligence or accuracy of belief among a large population, the average rank is the upper quartile. Individuals can of course err in self-assessment, but this result does not come from random error.

I want to express my personal thanks to the authors involved in this volume for a most illuminating and provocative discussion.

DISCUSSION

Following the presentation of the lecture and the commentaries, audience members were given the opportunity to ask questions. Below is the resulting discussion.

AUDIENCE MEMBER: From the point of view of your theory, bubbles collapse when more of the asset is supplied, but it is not obvious why that would occur suddenly. You would think there would be a constant incentive or maybe a constantly increasing incentive as the bubble grows, but why would it be abrupt? Is there an interpretation in terms of your theory of why the option value would suddenly disappear or something similar?

JOSÉ A. SCHEINKMAN: I thought about that in the context of specific examples. One of the things you observe in the dotcom bubble is that, even though lock-up dates were public information, prices often fell a lot when lock-ups expired. Everybody knew there was the possibility of a large increase in supply when the lock-up expired. It is possible that optimists initially thought: This company is so good that those insiders are not going to sell much. But when they found out the amounts insiders sold, they realized that their opinion that the company was so valuable was not correct. This is the hypothesis that Wei Xiong, Harrison Hong, and I raised in our paper, that when these dates occurred, people revalued their views about how much they actually know. Optimists surrendered when faced with the evidence of insiders' sale.

In the credit bubble, there are important events like the creation of synthetic CDOs. This was a big change, and evidently it was not easy to do it—this is the reason guys like Paulson made so much money. Michael Lewis relates an episode in *The Big Short* that speaks to this question.[1] A trader for Deutsche Bank, I believe, had bet against subprime mortgage bonds, but by April 2006 his superiors were worrying because the bonds he had shorted had in fact gone up in price. So the trader decided he needed others to join in and went around explaining why shorting subprime made sense. He succeeded, but it took him a while to find investors that wanted to join him.

SANFORD GROSSMAN: I'd like to elaborate a little bit on that and also to answer Professor Arrow's query about how can prices fall so far so rapidly in these situations. You have to understand what financial distress is like to a leveraged institution. Suppose you have borrowed to buy an asset to the point where you are levered 100 to 1—just to give you a simple example—and the underlying value goes down by just 1%. Then there is no collateral left and the lender— the bank—knows this, tries to seize the collateral.

Now, what is the lender going to do when it gets that collateral? If you are the only person who has the collateral, they will sell it and that is fine. They will get 99 cents instead of a dollar. Imagine that this is pervasive throughout the economy. All the lenders start getting this collateral and the market knows they are getting this collateral. Even before they ever try to sell the collateral, people will sell in front of them. If there is a lot of leverage, you can get a movement that is incredibly discontinuous, because of the knowledge that financial distress is going to lead to sales and everyone is then selling in front of this. You do not wait until the sale occurs before you are going to see the price fall; it just collapses around you. There are no bidders.

You should ask former professor Ben Bernanke, who went before Congress and testified that there are two notions of value. One is called the market or fire sale value of collateral. The other is called the basic value. The idea for the government to come in and buy assets that were being sold for distressed prices was based on the theory that, because of an extreme liquidity effect, these things are undervalued in the market and only the Fed has the liquidity to support the financial institutions' balance sheets that it liked. That was not the way the Fed put it, but that was the effect.

JOSÉ A. SCHEINKMAN: I want to elaborate on what Sandy said about leverage. I think one part of the puzzle is: who gives leverage? We can always tell a story that a person who gives leverage is insured by the government, has another source of money, whatever, which is probably true in some cases. It is hard to imagine that pessimists would be an important source of leverage, because they would be lending money guaranteed by an asset that they don't think is worth that much. In order to build a model that generates substantial leverage, you must have optimists that for some reason cannot hold an asset. In the credit crisis, as I have argued, it is easy to imagine it, but in other cases it may be harder to explain.

AUDIENCE MEMBER: I want to ask about the implications of these bubble environments. From a policy point of view, how does the policymaker know whether the Type A or Type B investor has the right view of the world, and how should policymaking be done in such an environment?

JOSÉ A. SCHEINKMAN: I protected myself by claiming that I didn't know how to answer this question fully during my talk. First, as I said, certain bubbles may be good. I believe that if you would look at the dotcom bubble, you may conclude that it was worth having it. Of course, people who lost money were not happy, but there are a lot of things we have today which are a result of the cheap capital provided to the Internet industry during the dotcom bubble. You could perhaps argue that Google wouldn't exist if it weren't for the dotcom bubble. So it is even harder for policy makers. They have to find out whether there's a bubble, but also to figure out the benefits—if any—of the bubble. However, they may establish policies that limit the extent of bubbles when they occur—remove barriers to shorting or impose limits on leverage, for instance.

JOSEPH E. STIGLITZ: In some sense, it is the externalities generated by the bubble with which we are concerned. It is the instances where behavior clearly has consequences for people other than those undertaking the risk. That is clearly the case not just when you have government-insured leverage, but also when there are banks that are "too big to fail" (or there is a belief that a bank is too big to fail). If there is a widespread belief that you will act as if it is too big to fail, then I think you have to stop the excessive leverage. That is a clear case where your actions have societal effects that the investor does not take into account.

AUDIENCE MEMBER: We have talked a lot about housing, but I think it is a pretty significant bubble that happened. I wanted to make a couple of observations, which call into question some of these assumptions. The first is, oddly enough, the places which had the biggest housing bubbles—defined as "you know it when you see it"—are places where supply is actually easiest to come online, places like Phoenix, Las Vegas, Miami, where condominiums were built. They are exactly the places where you would have thought supply was very difficult, but actually supply is very easy in those places. In a global context, it is markets like Spain, where again, supply was enormously easy to spare, not in markets where supply was very difficult.

The second is the ferocity of the decline in prices also ties very closely with leverage. If you look at the Spanish market, for example, it has kind of dribbled down, but by every sense, the run-up in prices in Spain was as severe as in prices elsewhere. Housing also does not have margin calls—the standard form for which you think about the effect of leverage on asset prices collapsing. Homeowners in Las Vegas and Phoenix did not get a margin call on their homes. They may have voluntarily walked away from them in some cases, but it was not driven by a margin call, though clearly leverage played a big role in some of those markets. And subprime loans were available in Texas, where we did not see bubbles.

I want to pose an idea at least that Internet companies produced stocks where it was very easy to produce a very big supply. It created a market where the supply was easy to produce as opposed to hard, and this may be the idea of monetization, the idea that you actually need some of it around in order to speculate. There may be something more to the idea that it is not just that supply bursts the bubble, unless it appears instantaneously. With the Internet bubble it seemed to, but I think when one looks at housing, there is a very different picture than some of the assumptions one might normally make to explain this.

JOSÉ A. SCHEINKMAN: Actually, there is a paper by Glaeser, Gyourko, and Saiz exactly on this topic. They argue that the real estate price bubbles in the '80s and in the recent period were more pronounced in places where supply is inelastic, especially in places where there was a lot of regulation. Bubbles did occur in elastic supply places but were much more short-lived.

Of course we can also think of a "bubble" in construction. Supply is going to grow more in the place where it's easier to build.

AUDIENCE MEMBER: What is striking about all these bubbles is that they always have at the very beginning something truthful, for example a technological innovation regarding the real estate bubble in Spain. At least that is the story that people tell, that there was a phenomenal potential for household formation in Spain due to the phenomenal youth unemployment that we saw in the previous years.

Somehow that featured not very prominently in this kind of beginning of the bubble, and I wanted to know your thoughts on the matter.

JOSÉ A. SCHEINKMAN: There is always some grain of truth, you're right, but we also need to explain why they get exacerbated. The argument I make for the origins of optimism is an attempt to explain this process of exaggeration.

JOSEPH E. STIGLITZ: I want to pick up the last set of comments that Ken made about the assumption of rationality and the role that it plays in macro-economic models and financial markets. In a way, it is illustrated by one part of José's comments on compensation schemes. Most of the compensation schemes rewarded executives the same whether they increased returns by increasing alpha or increasing beta. Those are clearly very different types of effort. Anybody can increase beta. Almost nobody can increase alpha. They had incentive structures that were in that sense fundamentally flawed.

Secondly, since the incentive structures were mostly related to stock market performance and stock market performance was related to the information that they disclosed, they had incentives to distort the information they supplied to the market, not just incentives for distorted risk-taking.

Thirdly, most of the incentive structures were not even tax efficient; that is, there were other ways of designing the compensation with the same incentive structure that reduced the sum of corporate and individual income tax.

I could go on with explaining how badly designed the incentive structures have been. A good incentive system should be able to "detect" when it is that profits are higher as a result of the manager's efforts, or when they are higher for other reasons. Basing compensation on relative performance does this, yet few firms employ such compensation schemes. The typical compensation scheme rewards managers for an increase in stock market value, regardless of the reason. But why should pay be dependent on how the stock market as a whole performs?

American capitalism has been based on very flawed incentive structures. Seeing this, you have to ask if you can really believe in the hypothesis of rationality I think the answer is clearly not. The observed incentive structures could be rational in the sense that given the *irrational* beliefs of other people, it might be rational for managers to behave in the way they did, because the market didn't penalize them for it and the market might penalize them for acting in a way that might seem more consistent with "rationality." A firm that used a *rational* incentive structure might not have been able to attract good managers. But at the core of the economy there is a degree of irrationality. It seems to me that the models that had become very dominant in macro-economics and finance that rest on rationality are very deeply flawed and are not likely to give us insights into how our actual economy behaves.

SANFORD GROSSMAN: I want to emphasize what Joe was saying, but maybe make it a little bit broader. Everything that Joe said in describing the flawed nature of incentives and financing in the private sector could also be said of the public sector. Witness the disastrous consequences over the last few years from the actions taken in the early 2000s by the Greek government. They used swaps to move "on-balance sheet" debt to an off-balance sheet obligation, and thus satisfy the Euro entry requirement to reduce their debt-to-GDP ratio to 50%.

Similarly, in the U.S., if we look at the period leading up to the crisis, the capital requirements that were applied to so-called too-big-to-fail institutions were negligible. It is very correct and easy to criticize the model we have of the rational behavior of consumers and investors, but it is as if once we get into regulatory matters, we are dealing with regulators as super-humans. It is easy to write a policy paper that attributes all kinds of defects in capitalism, because the private sector is populated by defective creatures named humans, who are not super-computers but actually pretty primitive organisms. But once those primitive organisms get into government, like when they go work for the New York Fed and are responsible for setting capital requirements, these imperfect organisms become super-human beings in the policy papers that economists write. That has always seemed strange to me, because there is very little genetic difference between somebody who prefers to work for Goldman Sachs or for the New York Fed or the Treasury. (As a matter of fact, there may be zero genetic difference, because it could be the same individual.)

Even barring that, this notion that there is such a thing called policy, which is done by policymakers who are organisms that are different from the incredibly imperfect creatures we write about, has always struck me as very strange. Why is it we have a different model of the organisms that are in government from the model we have of the organisms that are outside of government?

JOSEPH E. STIGLITZ: It is not that they are not any different in terms of their genetic composition. They have different incentives. Now sometimes those incentives do not work very well and they can have perverse effects, but they do have different incentives. One of the issues is what kind of incentive structures we can create in the public sphere and how the public sphere can change the incentive structures for the private sphere.

You are going to have rules of the game in both the public and private spheres, and somebody has to write those rules of the game. What we are really talking about is how those are written.

PATRICK BOLTON: I just want to make two points that have already been touched on, one in particular by Sanford, regarding leverage. It is hard to explain why there was so much leverage. Who would lend so much so recklessly? Part of the story is politics; the narrative of the crisis will have to be a political narrative. You cannot do everything, and José focused on the classical economic model, but I think if you want to understand the housing crisis, the very rapidly-growing leverage in government debt in the U.S., and the European debt crisis, politics will have to be part of the explanation.

I want to return to the question of what policy conclusions we can draw from all these analyses. It is very hard to draw any conclusions, but in my view, one thing definitely needs revisiting, and that is the way we structure pension savings in the U.S. based on the 401k model, where basically we encourage households to invest in a very high and speculative stock market. We may have to revisit that model of whether it makes sense to expose households to such enormous aggregate risk for the pension savings.

JOSÉ A. SCHEINKMAN: All I want to do is thank Ken, of course, and Sandy, Patrick, Joe, and the audience for listening to what I said and for very interesting criticism and comments. Thank you.

NOTES

SPECULATION, TRADING, AND BUBBLES

1. For example, Eugene Fama in Cassidy (2010) "I don't even know what a bubble means. These words have become popular. I don't think they have any meaning."
2. page S398.
3. A related definition of bubbles, which has been used in the literature, is of episodes in which buyers purchase an asset not on the basis of payoffs that the asset would generate, but because they intend to resell it at a higher price in the future (Brunnermeier (2008)).
4. For example, Blanchard and Watson (1983), Tirole (1985) or Santos and Woodford (1997).
5. For if everyone agrees on the value at T, rational investors would refuse to pay at time $T - 1$ any price above the discounted value at T. Thus there would be no bubble at time $T - 1$. Repeating this reasoning one concludes that a bubble never arises.
6. Shiller (2006).
7. Barberis, Shleifer and Vishny (1998), Daniel, Hirshleifer and Subrahmanyam (1998) and Gervais and Odean (2001) show how behavioral biases may generate such a feedback mechanism.

8. See section 2.3 for some examples.
9. Mackay (1932), page 51.
10. Neal (1990).
11. Garber (1980), pages 121–122.
12. Scott (1910-12), page 323.
13. Garber (1980), page 122.
14. Anderson was a clerk at the South Sea Company during the bubble (Harris (1994), page 615).
15. Cited in Murphy (1986), Chapter 9.
16. Anderson (1787), pages 102-103.
17. Davis et al. (2005).
18. Hong and Stein (2007).
19. For instance, in February 2000, Internet firms represented 6% of the public equity market but 19% of the trading volume (Ofek and Richardson (2003)).
20. This must be compared with an annual turnover of 100% for the typical NYSE stock at that time.
21. Ofek and Richardson (2003).
22. Janeway 2012.
23. Including so called Alt-A mortgage loans.
24. Thomas and Van Order (2010).
25. Synthetic CDOs have been blamed for the inordinate damage created by the subprime implosion (see, e.g., Nocera (2010) for a non-technical indictment of synthetics), because they allowed optimistic financial institutions to take even more subprime risks. However, it is not obvious what would have happened if synthetics had not existed. First, the price of "safe" subprime-based securities would have been higher, causing bigger losses per security albeit on a smaller number of securities. Second, and more scary, is that we would have ended up with an even larger number of unfinished houses in the Southwest.
26. Glaeser et al. (2006) argue that real estate bubbles are also deflated by increases in housing supply.

27. The lowest spreads for a 5-year CDS on Greek debt, in the single digits, were reached later, in January 2007.

28. In fact, U.S. regulations often require many institutional lenders to maintain the right to terminate a stock loan at any time (D'Avolio (2002)).

29. Related models of bubbles using differential information include Allen, Morris and Postlewaite (1993), Abreu and Brunnermeier (2003), and Conlon (2004).

30. That is, if J. C. emits an opinion, it is equally likely to be a "buy" or a "sell."

31. See Geanakoplos (2010) for a recent summary.

32. "The average coupon on subprime adjustable-rate mortgages was several hundred basis points above the comparable prime loans. And yet, if investors think that house prices can rise 11% per year, expected losses are minimal." (Foote et al. (2012) pages 32–33).

33. Optimistic investors also obtained leverage from financial market participants that understood the risks involved, but benefitted from skewed incentives.

34. During the dotcom period, so-called objective research firms with no investment banking business, such as Sanford and Bernstein, issued recommendations every bit as optimistic as investment banks (e.g. Cowen et al. (2006)).

35. Wolfe (1975), page 84.

36. See Holmstrom (2006) and Holmstrom and Kaplan (2001).

37. Or as Lewis (2004) wrote: "The investor cares about short-term gains in stock prices a lot more than he does about the long-term viability of a company. . . . The investor, of course, likes to think of himself as a force for honesty and transparency, but he has proved, in recent years, that he prefers a lucrative lie to an expensive truth. And he's very good at letting corporate management know it."

38. Froot et al. (1991) point out that the horizon of many institutional investors is around 1 year.

39. See Figure 1 in Xiong and Yu (2011).

APPENDIX: FORMAL MODEL

1. It would be easy to accommodate a non-stationary dividend.
2. That is, maximal variance.
3. However, see footnote 4, for an assumption that implies that insiders only sell.
4. Equivalently we could have assumed instead that the reservation price of insiders is greater than v_2^B, with probability π and less than $\delta\bar{\theta}$, with probability $1 - \pi$. For in this case, given that equation (14) and inequality (15) hold, insiders sell no shares with probability π and sell all their shares with probability $1 - \pi$.
5. A different rule, such as giving priority to agents in group A, would change the details of the computations that follow, but would not alter the result of interest.

FURTHER CONSIDERATIONS

1. Michael Lewis. 2010, *The Big Short: Inside the Doomsday Machine*, New York: W.W. Norton.

REFERENCES

Abreu, D., and M.K. Brunnermeier. 2003. "Bubbles and Crashes," *Econometrica*, 71(1): pages 173–204.

Allen, F. and D. Gale. 2002. "Optimal Financial Crises." *The Journal of Finance* 53 (4): pages 1245–1284.

Allen, F., S. Morris, and A. Postlewaite. 1993. "Finite Bubbles with Short Sale Constraints and Asymmetric Information," *Journal of Economic Theory*, 61(2): pages 206–229.

Alpert, M. and H. Raiffa. 1982. "A Progress Report on the Training of Probability Assessors." *Judgment under Uncertainty: Heuristics and Biases*. Pages 294–305.

Anderson, A. 1787. *An Historical; and Chronological Deduction of the Origin of Commerce*, vol. 3. London, UK.

Arrow, Kenneth J. 1951a. "An Extension of the Basic Theorems of Classical Welfare Economics." In *Proceedings of the Second Berkeley Symposium on Mathematical Statistics and Probability*, edited by J. Neyman, pages 507–532. Berkeley: University of California Press.

——. 1951b. *Social Choice and Individual Values*. New York: Wiley.

——. 1962a. "The Economic Implications of Learning by Doing." *Review of Economic Studies* 29: pages 155–173.

Arrow, Kenneth J., and F. Debreu. 1954. "Existence of an Equilibrium for a Competitive Economy." *Econometrica* 22: pages 265–290.

REFERENCES

Arrow, K.J. 1986. "Rationality of Self and Others in an Economic System." *Journal of Business*: Pages 385–399.

Barberis, N., Shleifer, A., and Vishny, R. 1998. "A model of investor sentiment." *Journal of Financial Economics*, 49 (3): pages 307–343.

Bebchuk, L.A. and J.M. Fried. 2006. *Pay without Performance: The Unfulfilled Promise of Executive Compensation*. Harvard University Press.

Ben-David, I., J.R. Graham, and C.R. Harvey. 2010. *Managerial Miscalibration*. Tech. rep., National Bureau of Economic Research.

Blanchard, O. and M. Watson 1983. *Bubbles, rational expectations and financial markets*, Tech. rep., National Bureau of Economic Research.

Bolton, P., J. Scheinkman, and W. Xiong. 2006. "Executive Compensation and Short-termist Behaviour in Speculative Markets." *The Review of Economic Studies* 73 (3): pages 577–610.

Brunnermeier, M.K. 2008. "Bubbles." In *The New Palgrave Dictionary of Economics*, edited by S. Durlauf and L. Blume. Basingstoke: Palgrave Macmillan.

Carlos, A., L. Neal, and K. Wandschneider. 2006. "Dissecting the Anatomy of Exchange Alley: The Dealings of Stockjobbers during and after the South Sea Bubble." Unpublished paper, University of Illinois.

Cassidy, J. 2010. "Rational Irrationality: An Interview with Eugene Fama." *The New Yorker*. November 1.

Cheng, I.H., H. Hong, and J. Scheinkman. 2010. "Yesterday's Heroes: Compensation and Creative Risk-Taking." *ECGI-Finance Working Paper* (285).

Conlon, J. R. 2004. "Simple Finite Horizon Bubbles Robust to Higher Order Knowledge," *Econometrica*, 72(3): pages 927–936.

Cooper, A.C., C.Y. Woo, and W.C. Dunkelberg. 1988. "Entrepreneurs' Perceived Chances for Success." *Journal of Business Venturing* 3 (2): pages 97–108.

Cowen, A., B. Groysberg, and P. Healy. 2006. "Which Types of Analyst Firms Are More Optimistic?" *Journal of Accounting and Economics* 41 (1): pages 119–146.

D'avolio, G. 2002. "The Market for Borrowing Stock." *Journal of Financial Economics* 66 (2): pages 271–306.

Davis, L.E., L.D. Neal, and E.N. White. 2005. *The Highest Price Ever: The Great NYSE Seat Sale of 1928–1929 and Capacity Constraints.* Tech. rep., National Bureau of Economic Research.

Daniel, K., Hirshleifer, D., and Subrahmanyam, A. 1998. "Investor psychology and security market under-and overreactions." *The Journal of Finance*, 53 (6): pages 1839-1885.

Diamond, P. 1965. "National Debt in a Neoclassical Growth Model." *American Economic Review* 55 (5): pages 1126–1150.

Diamond, P. 1967. "The Role of a Stock Market in a General Equilibrium Model with Technological Uncertainty." *American Economic Review* 57: pages 753–776.

Diether, K.B., C.J. Malloy, and A. Scherbina. 2002. "Differences of Opinion and the Cross Section of Stock Returns." *The Journal of Finance* 57 (5): pages 2113–2141.

Foote, C.L., K.S. Gerardi, and P.S. Willen. 2012. *Why Did So Many People Make so Many Ex Post Bad Decisions? The Causes of the Foreclosure Crisis.* Tech. rep., National Bureau of Economic Research.

Friedman, M. 1966. *Essays in Positive Economics*, vol. 231. University of Chicago Press.

Froot, K.A., A.F. Perold, and J.C. Stein. 1991. *Shareholder Trading Practices and Corporate Investment Horizons.* Tech. rep., National Bureau of Economic Research.

Garber, P. 1980. *Famous First Bubbles: The Fundamentals of Early Mania.* Cambridge, MA: MIT Press, 1st ed.

Geanakoplos, J. 2010. "The Leverage Cycle." *NBER Macroeconomics Annual* 24 (1): pages 1–66.

Gervais, S., & Odean, T. 2001. "Learning to be overconfident." *Review of Financial Studies*, 14 (1): pages 1–27.

Glaeser, E.L., J.E. Gyourko, and R.E. Saks. 2006. "Urban Growth and Housing Supply." *Journal of Economic Geography* 6 (1): pages 71–89.

Glaeser, E.L., J.E. Gyourko, and A. Saiz. 2008. "Housing Supply and Housing Bubbles," Harvard Institute of Economic Research Discussion Paper No. 2158. Available at SSRN: http://ssrn.com/abstract=1169182 or http://dx.doi.org/10.2139/ssrn.1169182

Greenwald, B, and J. E. Stiglitz. 1986. "Externalities in Economies with Imperfect Information and Incomplete Markets." *Quarterly Journal of Economics* 1 (2): pages 229–264.

Grossman, S.J., and J.E. Stiglitz. 1980. "On the Impossibility of Informationally Efficient Markets." *The American Economic Review*, American Economic Association Vol. 70 (3, Jun): pages 393–408.

Harris, R. 1994. "The Bubble Act: Its Passage and Its Effects on Business Organization." *The Journal of Economic History* 54 (3): pages 610–627.

Harrison, J.M., and D.M. Kreps. 1978. "Speculative Investor Behavior in a Stock Market with Heterogeneous Expectations." *The Quarterly Journal of Economics* 92 (2): pages 323–336.

Holmstrom, B. 2006. *Pay without Performance and the Managerial Power Hypothesis: A Comment. Available at SSRN 899096.*

Holmstrom, B., and S.N. Kaplan. 2001. *Corporate Governance and Merger Activity in the U.S.: Making Sense of the 1980s and 1990s.* Tech. rep., National Bureau of Economic Research.

Hong, H., and J.C. Stein. 2007. "Disagreement and the Stock Market." *The Journal of Economic Perspectives* 21 (2): pages 109–128.

Hong, H., J. Scheinkman, and W. Xiong. 2006. "Asset Float and Speculative Bubbles." *The Journal of Finance* 61 (3): pages 1073–1117.

———. 2008. "Advisors and Asset Prices: A Model of the Origins of Bubbles." *Journal of Financial Economics* 89 (2): pages 268–287.

Janeway, W. 2012. *Doing Capitalism in the Innovation Economy.* Cambridge, UK: Cambridge University Press, 1st ed.

Kidd, J.B. 1970. "The Utilization of Subjective Probabilities in Production Planning." *Acta Psychologica* 34: pages 338–347.

Kindleberger, C.P., and R. Aliber. 1978. *Manias, Panics, and Crashes: A History of Financial Crises,* Hoboken, NJ: John Wiley & Sons, 2000.

Lamont, O.A., and R.H. Thaler. 2003. "Can the Market Add and Subtract? Mispricing in Tech Stock Carve-outs." *Journal of Political Economy*, 111 (2): pages 227–268.

Lewis, M. 2004. "The Irresponsible Investor." *New York Times Magazine*. June 6.

Mackay, C. 1932. *Extraordinary Popular Delusions and the Madness of Crowds*. New York: Farrar, Straus and Giroux.

Mei, J., J.A. Scheinkman, and W. Xiong. 2009. "Speculative Trading and Stock Prices: Evidence from Chinese AB Share Premia." *Annals of Economics and Finance* 10 (2): pages 225–255.

Mill, J.S. 1848. *Principles of Political Economy with Some of Their Applications to Social Philosophy*. Indianapolis, IN: Hackett Publishing. 2004.

Morgenstern, O., and J. Van Neumann. 1944. *Theory of Games and Economic Behavior*. Princeton NJ: Princeton Univ. Press. 2004.

Murphy, A.E. 1986. *Richard Cantillon: Entrepreneur and Economist*. Clarendon Press Oxford.

Neal, L. 1990. *The Rise of Financial Capitalism: International Capital Markets in the Age of Reason*. Cambridge, UK: Cambridge University Press.

Nocera, J. 2010. "A Wall Street Invention Let the Crisis Mutate." *New York Times*. April 17:B1.

Ofek, E., and M. Richardson. 2003. "Dotcom Mania: The Rise and Fall of Internet Stock Prices." *The Journal of Finance* 58 (3): pages 1113–1138.

Samuelson, P.A. 1958. "An Exact Consumption-Loan Model of Interest with or without the Social Contrivance of Money." *Journal of Political Economy*, University of Chicago Press, vol. 66: page 467.

Santos, M.S., and M. Woodford. 1997. "Rational Asset Pricing Bubbles." *Econometrica*: pages 19–57.

Savage, L.J. 1954. *Foundations of Statistics*. New York: Dover Publications. 1972.

Scheinkman, J.A. and W. Xiong. 2003. "Overconfidence and Speculative Bubbles." *Journal of Political Economy* 111 (6): pages 1183–1219.

REFERENCES

Scott, W.R. 1910-12. *The Constitution and Finance of English, Scottish and Irish Joint-Stock Companies by 1720,* vol. 3. Cambridge, UK: Cambridge University Press.

Shiller, R.J. 2006. *Irrational Exuberance.* Crown Business.

Stiglitz, J. 1982. "The Inefficiency of the Stock Market Equilibrium." *Review of Economic Studies* 49 (2): pages 241–261.

Tetlock, P.E. 2005. *Expert Political Judgment: How Good Is It? How Can We Know?* Princeton University Press.

Tirole, J. 1985. "Asset bubbles and overlapping generations." *Econometrica* 53 (6): pages 1499–1528.

Thomas, J., and R. Van Order. 2010. "Housing Policy, Subprime Markets and Fannie Mae and Freddie Mac: What We Know, What We Think We Know and What We Don't Know." In *St. Louis FRB Conference.*

Wolfe, T. 1975. *The Painted Word.* New York: Farrar, Straus and Giroux.

Xiong, W., and J. Yu. 2011. "The Chinese Warrants Bubble." *American Economic Review* 101: pages 2723–2753.

Yan, H. 2008. "Natural Selection in Financial Markets: Does It Work?" *Management Science* 54 (11):pages 1935–1950.

NOTES ON CONTRIBUTORS

KENNETH J. ARROW is a Nobel Laureate in Economic Sciences and Professor Emeritus at Stanford University. He was awarded the Nobel Prize in 1972 "for pioneering contributions to general economic equilibrium theory and welfare theory." Arrow began his graduate study in economics and statistics at Columbia University, earning his Ph.D. there. He has held positions on the Cowles Commission for Research in Economics, at the University of Chicago, Harvard University, and Stanford University. His research, apart from social choice theory, has focused on general economic equilibrium. The profound transformation of the general equilibrium theory is marked by his groundbreaking work. He helped open new productive paths for research in this area, and in so doing, has made fundamental contributions to the renewal of the theory.

PATRICK BOLTON is the Barbara and David Zalaznick Professor of Business at Columbia Business School and Professor of Economics at Columbia University. He has worked at the University of California at Berkeley, Harvard University, C.N.R.S. Laboratoire d' Economét-rie de L'Ecole Polytechnique, the London School of Economics, the Institut d'Etudes Europénnes de l'Université Libre de Bruxelles, and Princeton University. His research interests are in contract theory and contracting issues in corporate finance and industrial organization. His work in industrial organization focuses on antitrust economics and the potential anticompetitive effects of various contracting practices. Professor Bolton also served as founding director of the Institute for Advanced Study in Toulouse. He published his first book, *Contract Theory*, with Mathias Dewatripont and co-edited a second book with Howard Rosenthal, *Credit Markets for the Poor*. His third book was recently published by Columbia University press, co-edited with Joseph Stiglitz and Frederic Samama: *Sovereign Wealth Funds and Long-Term Investing*.

SANFORD J. GROSSMAN earned his B.A. in 1973, M.A. in 1974 and Ph.D. in 1975, all in Economics, from the University of Chicago. Since receiving his doctorate, he has held academic appointments at Stanford University, the University of Chicago, Princeton University (as the John L. Weinberg Professor of Economics, 1985–89), and the University of Pennsylvania's Wharton School of Business. At Wharton, Dr. Grossman held the position of Steinberg Trustee Professor of Finance from 1989 to 1999 (a title now held in Emeritus) and also served as the Director of the Wharton Center for Quantitative Finance (1994–1999). Dr. Grossman's original contributions to economic research received official recognition when he was awarded the John Bates Clark Medal in 1987. Dr. Grossman currently serves as Chairman and Chief Executive Officer of QFS Asset Management, L.P.

JOSÉ A. SCHEINKMAN is the Edwin W. Rickert Professor of Economics at Columbia University and Theodore A. Wells '29 Professor of Economics Emeritus at Princeton University. From 1973 until 1999 he held appointments at the University of Chicago where he was Alvin H. Baum Distinguished Service Professor of Economics (1997–1999) and Chairman of Department of Economics (1995–1998). Scheinkman is a member of the National Academy of Sciences, a Fellow of the American Academy of Arts and Sciences, a Corresponding Member of the Brazilian Academy of Sciences, a Fellow of the Econometric Society, a recipient of a *docteur honoris causa* from the Université Paris-Dauphine, and a recipient of the John Simon Guggenheim Memorial Fellowship (2007). He was co-editor of the *Journal of Political Economy.*

JOSEPH E. STIGLITZ is University Professor at Columbia University, the winner of the 2001 Nobel Memorial Prize in Economics, and a lead author of the 1995 IPCC report, which shared the 2007 Nobel Peace Prize. He is co-chair of the Committee on Global Thought. He was chairman of the U.S. Council of Economic Advisors under President Clinton and chief economist and senior vice president of the World Bank from 1997 through 2000. Stiglitz received the John Bates Clark Medal, awarded biennially to the American economist under 40 who has made the most significant contribution to the subject. He was a Fulbright Scholar at Cambridge University, held the Drummond Professorship at All Souls College Oxford, and has also taught at M.I.T, Yale, Stanford, and Princeton.

INDEX